The
FLAME
That
TRANSFORMS

As we cannot live without air, so we cannot do without light.

Mohandas K. Gandhi

Darkness cannot drive out darkness, only light can do that.

Martin Luther King, Jr.

I look to the diffusion of light and education as the resource most to be relied on for ameliorating the condition, promoting the virtue and advancing the happiness of man.

Thomas Jefferson

I warmly commend the installation of the World Peace Flame at the Peace Palace in The Hague during this time when peace is so crucial to the future of humanity.

President, European Parliament

This is a living symbol of peace. It is a really worthwhile thing you are doing and I invite you now to bring the World Peace Flame to the UN in Geneva.

former UN High Commissioner for Human Rights

The fact that someone can make something like this happen in the first place is a miracle—regardless of what comes next! I have seen the miracles which happen around the World Peace Flame and the Life Foundation and I can only highly recommend them to you.

former Member of the European Parliament

In his speech earlier this year his Holiness declared his wish that '…this Jubilee year would be a year of reconciliation and unity…' The Pontificate at The Vatican accepted the World Peace Flame in this capacity when in June 2000 the World Peace Flame was presented to Pope John Paul II as a symbol of the unity we are all striving for.

His Holiness Pope John Paul II

When historians in London told Mahatma Gandhi that nowhere in history had non-violence ever succeeded, he replied, 'Don't worry, Gentlemen, I am making history.' This eternal World Peace Flame is making history. When we each can embrace the possibility that peace already exists, and when all our actions are based on compassion, then this peace will become a living reality.

Savitri MacCuish, World Peace Flame Foundation

The World Peace Flame is a magnificent symbol—a symbol of peace, unity, freedom and truth. It reminds us of the essential freedom of the human spirit to create peace at any time, under any circumstances. You may ask, 'Why should such a small flame as this have such a great impact?' I would say, 'Why not? Why should we not find the secret of the ocean in a drop of water or the secret of light inside a tiny flame?'

Dr Mansukh Patel, Co-Founder, Life Foundation

This groundswell of support for the profound significance of the World Peace Flame will conflagrate hearts, fire souls and fuel feet to join the march of humanity's movement towards world peace. Indeed, it is a forerunner of its fulfillment.

Author, Founder, International Spiritual Centre, Los Angeles

The World Peace Flame is an important symbol of the Parliament's goals of peace, equality and open dialogue.

World Parliament of Religions

Those who were at the ceremony of the World Peace Flame witnessed a moment of great symbolism. The World Peace Flame unites ancient and modern cultures by expressing the fundamental aspiration of both—the hope of peace! This Flame will burn brightly, fuelled by the will of twenty million Australians.

former Federal Minister, Australia

I warmly welcome the World Peace Flame initiative. The challenges facing humanity demand that we all raise our voices in the cause of peace and dedicate ourselves to seeking constitutional answers to the world's problems and to avoid resorting to the force of arms... I congratulate everyone involved in this initiative and wish it every success.

Party Leader, The National Assembly for Wales

There is no more critical time in our modern history—with violence spinning out of control in the Middle East, Africa, parts of Europe and other hot spots—for us to rededicate ourselves to the cause of peace. Let this Flame inspire within us indignation towards violence as a tool of diplomacy in the world order and let us have the courage to speak out forcefully and with tenacity against those who perpetuate violence in the name of national interest.

Judge, Memphis, USA

Just as the night sky is made glorious by a thousand stars, so our times of darkness can become radiant with transformation by a thousand acts of positivity. The World Peace Flame reminds us all that 'we do make a difference'.

Andrew Wells
Director, International Projects, Life Foundation

This is a great honour—I shall always remember this day.

former President of Germany,
on receiving the World Peace Flame

I have known light in its purity and I consider it my duty to strive after it.

Johann Wolfgang von Goethe

THE
FLAME
THAT
TRANSFORMS

60 Empowering Stories of Hope, Courage and Inspiration

Savitri MacCuish
Mansukh Patel
Andrew Wells

 Life Foundation Publications, UK

First published in the United Kingdom by
Life Foundation Publications,
Nant Ffrancon, Bethesda, Bangor, North Wales LL57 3LX
E-mail: enquiries@lifefoundation.org.uk
www.lifefoundation.org.uk

ISBN - 1 873606 23 0

Printed by Biddles Ltd,
Woodbridge Park Estate
Woodbridge Road
Guildford, Surrey GU1 1DA, UK

Cover design by Felimy McArdle
Heleen van der Sanden and Samia Begum

Life Foundation Publications

P lant
A Tree

For every title published we plant and care for a tree

Printed on acid-free paper derived from
sustainable forests.

I dedicate this book to all who helped make the
World Peace Flame possible. In particular, I salute the role of
Colonel Harts and his colleagues in the Royal Netherlands
Air Force, and the Life Foundation teams in North Wales and
The Netherlands. My deepest respect and admiration to you
all for your breadth of vision and determination to
make the impossible possible.

Savitri

With the greatest reverence, I honour the presence of the
Flame that burns within each one of us. May it transform our
vision, ignite our dreams, and help us kindle the flame that
lies within ourselves and everyone we meet. May this shining
inner presence unite us all as one human family across all
barriers of creed, class, race and religion until we reach the
eventual goal—peace on this earth.

Mansukh

Humanity's great pioneers of truth so often describe
the highest goal in terms of light. I dedicate this book to all
who follow their radiant examples—to our friends in
America, Australia and Europe who have made it their life's
work to create pathways for others to follow— and to everyone who has contributed a message within these pages.
You are showing us all the way.

Andrew

What is the World Peace Flame?

In July, 1999, for the first time in history, seven flames of peace were flown across the oceans from five continents and united to create a single World Peace Flame in North Wales, UK.

Lit by eminent peacemakers, carried by military air forces and commercial airlines, the seven flames each represented the highest intentions for peace within their continents. The resulting World Peace Flame thus represents the combined aspirations for peace of humanity as a whole.

Since its inception, more than ten million people have taken candles lit from the World Peace Flame into their homes, workplaces or communities.

Eternally burning World Peace Flames have been installed in The Netherlands, outside the United Nations International Court of Justice in The Hague, and in Memphis, Tennessee, USA, within the National Civil Rights Museum.

It has been taken into war zones, included in peace negotiations and is present as a quiet witness to peace and healing in hospitals, churches, temples and civic buildings around the world.

You are invited to take a light from the World Peace Flame yourself. Use it as a reminder of your own highest purpose and potential, and your own ability to make a positive contribution to life. Please pass it on to others as a gesture of your friendship, care and respect.

The World Peace Flame aims to inspire people everywhere to create their own unique and valuable initiatives for creating a better world. You are welcome to visit the World Peace Flame at its home in the Life Foundation International Course Centre in Snowdonia, North Wales, UK.

www.worldpeaceflame.com

Contents

Acknowledgements i
Foreword v

Why Light?

    Understanding Light & the World Peace Flame 1
    How to Get the Most Out of this Book 7
    (Important Safety Considerations)

Part 1: Igniting the Fire -
The Origin of the World Peace Flame

Birth of an Idea—The Call of Light

    The Origin of the World Peace Flame 14
    A Legacy of Fertile Ground 16
    Ignition—The Birth of an Idea 22

The Journeys of the Flames:

Europe—The Royal Light of Europe

    The First Lighting 30
    The Quest to Fly the Flames .33
    Arrival 39

Africa—On the First Day

    Encounter at the Border 42
    Home to the Cradle of Humanity 46

A Dream Stronger than the Wind 49

America—'America the Beautiful'

'... For Purple Mountain Majesties' 52
Carrying the Flame 56

Canada—Bridging Three Nations

Anything Is Possible 60

Australasia—The Spirit Has Landed

Appearance of an Ancient Fire 64
The Six Day Journey 69

India—From Mahatma Gandhi

From a Poor Man's Broom .72
A Constant Stream of Certainty 75

Middle East—The Seventh Light

With Only Hours to Spare .80
On the Sands of Bahrain 83

The Birth of the World Peace Flame

30th July, 1999 88
The Joining of the Flames 90

Part 2: Empowering Stories of Hope, Courage and Inspiration

The Secret Power of Light

My Parachute Jump 98
The Lamplighters 103
The Day I Became Invincible 105
Civilisation 109
Why Not Me? 112

Encounter with a Miner 116
Sixty Days to the End of the War 119

Designing My Success

From the Factory Floor 124
The Switch 127
At the Pentagon 129
The Flame with a Mind of Its Own 133
Keepers of the Flame 136
Stroke Patient on a Neurology Ward 139
The Lighter Side of Life 142
Did You Get What You Asked For? 147
At the European Parliament 149
Journey of a Sacred Flame 153

Healing ~ Overcoming Tragedy

A Flame for Auschwitz 164
Baptism of Sunlight 168
After My Son Died 171
Rock Fall in a Coal Mine 177
Rabbit 181
Call to Action 183

With Children and the Family

How To Win at Football 188
Peace Begins at Home 191
Jimmy and the Peace Flame 192
When I Learned to Love My Mother 194
'Make Sure No-one Ever Stops You' 198
Healing Arguments in Our Relationship 200
The Girl with Special Needs 201
Feeling Warm Inside 205

At Work or Study

Within the Doctor's Surgery 208
A Remarkable Exam Result 212

End to Bullying .... .214
Ice Creams on Fire .... .217
The Film that Stopped the Rain .... .218
The Tax Inspection .... .222

Creating Unity and a Team that Excels

A Shopping List for Kosovo .... .228
A Team Creates Its Leadership .... .232
The Fellowship of the Flame .... .235
How Do You Forgive a War? .... .241

Part 3: Practical Ways to Use the World Peace Flame

Using the World Peace Flame

Using the World Peace Flame .... .248
Talisman for Self Empowerment .... .252

Meditations with Light—Healing Crises, Achieving Dreams

Meditations with Light .... .256
The World Peace Flame Meditation .... .258
What Should I Do Next? .... .260
Please Reveal Yourself to Me .... .262
Is There Anyone There Who Can Help Me? ...... .265

The World Peace Flame and You

The Ongoing Journey .... .270
Epilogue—The World Peace Flame and You .... .273
World Peace Flame Presentations .... .288
What Are Your Experiences with Light? .... .290
Contact Us .... .291
Introducing the Authors .... .292
Appendix—Using Candles Safely .... .295

Acknowledgements

L
ike the World Peace Flame itself, which was instigated in the unbelievably short time of three and a half months, this book has also only required a few short months to make the transformation from a large folder of ideas into a finished volume.

These wonderful results were only possible through the prodigious efforts of hundreds of people.

Firstly, how would any of our work be possible without the fertile ground prepared by Mansukh's parents, Chhaganbhai and Ecchaben Patel? Dear friends, you didn't live to see the fruit of your dream, yet we know your vision of peace is growing stronger every year.

The journeys of the Flames

This book rests above all upon the extraordinary efforts of all who helped establish the light of the World Peace Flame. Pushpaben Patel, Lalita Doerstel and Ganga Marvin, thank you for helping to catalyse the dialogue that gave birth to the World Peace Flame.

Thank you to Irene van Lippe Biesterfeld, Colonel Harts, Major de Ruyter and the Royal Netherlands Air Force for making the journey of the European Flame possible. Trudy and Thé de Ruyter, Nanna Coppens, Quirine and Hans Wentink, Ger, Jeannette and Bertram van Alphen thank you for your endless work, and also to Kamala Wood, and the Lord Mayor of Birmingham for welcoming the Flame to Britain.

For the African Flame—Paulette Agnew, Peter and Jenny Legge and Anita Goswami, how can we thank you for all your intricate preparations? Jane and Joseph Kanuthia, Heather Clements, and the crew from the South African Air Force, as well as the Lord Mayor of Oxford, you all helped us achieve a dream stronger than the wind.

To all who helped with the American Flame, perched amongst your 'purple mountain majesty', we send our gratitude for your support, particularly Jeannie Katz and Ron and Deb Houseman. And to Ned Hartfiel and Lalita, you gave everything to make the light shine brightly.

Thank you to Lalita and the Dutch Air Force for the journey of the Canadian Flame. Chief Stan Williams, Marie-Rose Stone and Norma Spence of the Ojibwa Nation, and Phil Lane Jr., thank you for teaching us about Light.

For the Australian Flame, Cherry Knight and Trish Brown have masterminded so much. And to Pearl Wymarra, Joseph Buhagia from the Sydney Olympic Committee, Estelle, the representatives of the Dharug Community—Leanne and Shay Tobin and Jackamarra—Wendy Holland, Mayor Rex Stubbs and the commanders from the RAAF as well as the Mayor of Swindon, thank you for kindling Australia's ancient Flame and carrying it with such care.

For the Indian Flame, Thakor Patel, Falguni, Meetha, Kasiram and Sita Patel, our appreciation for your courage. Ganga, and Ian and your team at Sri Lankan Airlines, thank you for your endless resourcefulness. To Joshna Patel and Helena Waters, to the Mayor of Hounslow and to all at the Swami Narayan Temple in Neasden, thank you for welcoming the light.

And for the Seventh Light, from the Middle East, thank you to all the teams in the RAF, and to Derek and Stef Robertson for your magnificent persistence.

To the British airport authorities, as well as all the airlines who really wanted to fly flames at the time and made great strides towards satisfying all the stringent safety regulations, we value the effort you made for peace. Special thanks to South African Airways for flying the Flame back to Africa.

Thanks to all who have at one point or another worked with the Life Foundation and have now gone on to other areas of working for World Peace. We salute you for your ideas and efforts, and for your compassion and humility.

A big thank you to the leaders and teams of Life Foundation in Scotland, Maristowe, London, Netherlands, North America, India and Australia for your amazing dedication and contribution to changing countless lives from despair to hope and darkness to light.

In culmination, our undying appreciation to Julie Hotchkiss, for co-ordinating so much, and to Annie Jones, Chris Barrington, John Jones and Rita Goswami for preparing the way.

'The Flame that Transforms'

Few things make your life more worthwhile than friendship, love and extraordinary teamwork, and this book has been filled with them all.

Firstly, we send our love and gratitude to the visionaries and leaders who have added their pen to the *Flame that Transforms*, as well as to everyone who has contributed stories and quotes to the book—you are our inspiration. Thank you all for being the pioneers of light.

Our thanks to all in the book team: Kate Couldwell, our immense gratitude for your hours of editing; Samia Begum, for your dramatic and artistic flair; Nanna Coppens and Ineke de Hulster for finding the Flame stories; and Robbie Schussig for being at the computer endlessly. Thanks to Sheila Roberts, Bridget Batchelor, Stef Robertson for your marvellous editing, and to Anne Smale, Chantal Savelkoul, Gwyneth Clapham, Shona Sutherland, Julie Seth, Jane McKee, Joan Groves, Ruth

Boaler, Vickie Brewster and Inez Kotterman for your help in compiling and proofing.

And Felimy McArdle, our endlessly patient graphic design-er, you are a hero and an inspiration to us. Few could do so much with your limitations in movement. Thanks also to Heleen van der Sanden, Kathi Dunn, Jane Clapham and Kamala Wood for your ideas.

Umed and Pushpa Patel, thank you for being endlessly there and perpetuating Mum and Dad's vision.

And finally, thank you to all in the Life Foundation for keep-ing the show moving while we have been absorbed with *The Flame that Transforms*.

Thank you for carrying on the dream.

Foreword

Mark Victor Hansen

I want to thank you personally for picking up this extraordinary book, because you are holding in your hands a vital key for bringing massive joy into your own life while helping peace break out across the world.

Many of you will know me as that *Chicken Soup for the Soul* guy, but I hope you'll see that as just part of my story. Behind and beyond the *Chicken Soup* phenomenon, my greatest passion is helping people transform our world into a better place.

I first met Mansukh Patel, Savitri MacCuish and Andrew Wells in a breakfast meeting that changed my life. The task we gave ourselves was to come up with a way to catalyse peace, not just in ourselves, not just in our families and workplaces, but also in our entire nations and the world. As we talked, these three dynamic authors introduced me to the World Peace Flame and described how millions of people are using its light as a reminder of the immense potential that lies within us all.

Two hours later we had set in motion a process that will one day light millions of candles and revector the direction of the world. *The Flame that Transforms* shows you how you can be a part of that process.

The World Peace Flame is a launching pad to your own illumination. Within each and every one of us there is a living flame, a beacon of our own inner joy, freedom and success. The World Peace Flame gives us a metaphor and a means for passing out this light, kindling the same radiance in others, and creating a wave that will wrap the world alight in peace.

I believe that today we are living through the biggest and fastest-moving turning point in history. If we look into the future we see two clear choices—a path of darkness containing tragic, horrific wars, or a path of brightness leading to the most beautiful, elegant, radiant peace. One is bountiful with opportunity, the other dangerous with weaponry. Which will *you* choose?

When Michelangelo completed his masterpiece, David, he was asked how he did it. 'I sculpted out everything that was not David,' he replied. *The Flame that Transforms* helps you discover that you are also a masterpiece, an inspired self-illuminated human being capable of propagating waves of joy, peace and success across the world.

The stories in this book will pick you up and put you back on the high wire of your life. For instance in 'Why Not Me?' you'll see that the whole of life is geared to reminding you just how much potential you have. I loved 'From the Factory Floor' because it echoes my own life's experience of teaching people that they *can* achieve anything, and once you've finished 'How Do You Forgive a War?' you'll fall in love again with every single human being on the planet.

I've worked all my life to eradicate poverty and to heal our world. The UN says that for the first time in history we have the means to bring real physical and economic success to every single human being. We have within our hands the ability to change the direction and destination of our planet so that it works for 100% of humanity.

There have never been greater opportunities for change. There has never been a greater need for action. As far as I'm concerned either war is obsolete or humanity is, and I am doing everything I can to help an epidemic of peace break out that crosses every border on the globe.

Once you open this book and read the stories within it your life will never be the same. Pick up a World Peace Flame today and use its light to fire your passion with the infinite potential you have within you, right now. You too can be a 'Flame that Transforms' and bring more joy to your own life, the people around you and to the world—today.

Mark Victor Hansen

Co-creator, No. 1 New York Times *best-selling series* Chicken Soup for the Soul ®
Co-author, The One Minute Millionaire

WHY LIGHT?

Introducing the
World Peace Flame

---

*" For the rest of my life, I want to
reflect on what light is. "*

Albert Einstein

Why Light?

Within these pages lies a treasury of stories of people's experiences with light. They have been chosen to inspire you, bring comfort in difficult times, make you laugh and maybe even make you cry with the humanity they express. Some of the stories describe unforgettable moments that have changed a person's life for ever. Others describe simple, silent moments that have given an ordinary life an extra sparkle. And, above all, their aim is to show how light can help you, too, discover new personal strengths that are truly awesome in their power.

The World Peace Flame

Most of the stories in this book relate to an extraordinary eternal flame that is being passed around the world from person to person.

It is called the World Peace Flame, and since its creation in July 1999, more than ten million candles and lamps have been lit from it. They have shone in homes and workplaces, hospitals and schools, places of worship and civic buildings. It has also been received by world leaders, taken into war zones and lit by politicians in peace negotiations. Most of all, it is helping people find greater healing, inner peace and purpose.

Why? What is so special about the World Peace Flame, and the light of Flames derived from it?

The answer lies in the response to an even greater question: Why have we human beings—in almost every culture since the dawn of history—used light to help guide us towards accessing our highest potential, our highest goal?

This book can inspire you to discover this potential, and learn how a living flame—and also its counterpart, the natural, radiant light of the sun—can help unleash immense reserves of energy, joy and clear wisdom within you.

Let us begin by discovering the power of light.

What does light do for us?

Right now, as you are holding this book, the degree to which you are receiving light will be influencing your body, mind and emotions to a profound extent.

❖ *At a physical level,* light is helping your body build reserves of vitamin D. After entering your eyes it stimulates your pineal gland and orchestrates more than a hundred physiological functions in a daily rhythm. When all these processes are in balance, you feel great, energised and full of zest. Exposure to full-spectrum light[1] has been shown to help ease premenstrual syndrome, obesity, osteoporosis, diabetes, and possibly even cancer and heart disease… Quite an impressive list!

❖ *At an emotional level,* the signals light is sending to your pineal gland also regulate the balance of 'feel good factors' such as melatonin and serotonin, freeing you from feelings of depression or despair in life.

❖ *At a mental level,* an adequate exposure to light, in the form of a candle flame or the sun, helps create a background state of clarity and positivity. When your phys-

---

[1] Most artificial sources of light do not contain all the frequencies our eyes use to send cues about the daily cycle to our brain. We can get these cues from natural daylight and, in many cases, from the glow of a flame.

iology and emotions are balanced and you are feeling
full of energy, your powers of discrimination become
sharpened and your perceptions more positive. This in
turn helps you to make better decisions, and so you
respond more effectively to people and invite better
responses back. The result is optimum success all
round. As you think, so you become…

❖   *And within your awareness*, most importantly of all, light
can direct you towards the same source of strength that
every culture in history has said exists within us all: a
radiant experience of light that brings us equanimity,
peace and bubbling inner joy.

What the World Peace Flame brings to your life

So, when you hold a lamp or candle lit from the World Peace
Flame its golden light helps configure your body, your emotions and your mind for success. It is a reminder of your highest goals and strengths, and helps you let go of stress, uncer-
tainty and fear.

And it brings you much more than that.

It brings the collective strengths and pure intent of all who
are using the light of the World Peace Flame.

It brings a reminder of hope, of peace.

And most of all, it helps remind us all that we have a unique
and valuable part to play in creating a world in which we
respect the environment, care for people and strive to achieve
our innermost aspirations.

Please pass on the World Peace Flame

The World Peace Flame has been passed on from individual to
individual, spreading like the rays of the sun into every continent. It has connected millions of people who will never know
each other personally.

When we give a World Peace Flame to another person, it is a way of expressing our care, our respect and our friendship.

The whole is greater than the sum of the parts

Each of these single acts may not seem as though they change the world. Yet when countless people do the same, the sum of all these gestures adds up to something very powerful.

They add up to a world at peace.

Light a World Peace Flame and pass it on to others. It will create a source of light to help bring healing, joy and new strengths into your life and the lives of many others.

" *Just as the greatest source of power in the physical universe comes from its tiniest component—the atom,*

So the greatest power in society comes from its smallest component—the individual. "

Laurens van der Post

When I gaze into the Flame that has its origins in the seven corners of the world, I feel the forces of purity and unity that otherwise are buried under the weight of headline news or conflicts.

The uniqueness of the World Peace Flame is that these seven Flames, after coming together to form a single Flame in North Wales, have now been dispersed to every corner of the globe, like gold dust in the sunshine.

My pupils and patients feel the benefit of the Flame's ability to reach the very centre of their innate nature.

General Practitioner, Scotland

How to Make the Most of this Book

In three fascinating parts

The first part of this book is the story of the creation of the World Peace Flame. It tells how ordinary people across the world, peacemakers, military personnel and community leaders all played a part in turning a single, extraordinary idea into a reality. It is a dramatic story with an enchanting conclusion.

The second part of the book brings you stories of people who have used the power of light to find healing, discover untapped strengths and regain self-worth, joy and love. All are stories of real people whose lives have been painted in extraordinary colour by the artist's brush of light.

And in the third part you will find techniques to help you benefit from the power of light and use the World Peace Flame to its maximum potential.

Choosing which story to read

Some people may like to sit down and read this book from cover to cover.

However, most will prefer to use it as a 'dip-in' book. Choose a story at random, leaf through the sections or titles until you find something that catches your eye, or even take a quiet moment to choose the story or page that you sense is most appropriate for you. Whatever method you use we know you will find something that speaks to your heart.

About the stories in this book

All the stories in this book are true. They have happened to real people living real lives. In some of the stories in Part 2 we have changed names, places and minor details to protect the privacy of the people involved.

The stories have all been written by the authors, and are based on interviews and written material supplied by people close to the incidents described.

Many of these people have made the World Peace Flame so much a part of their life that they have experienced many inspiring and transforming incidents. Consequently, in a couple of cases, we have included more than one story per person.

Important Safety and Health Considerations

Most of the stories related in this book encourage you to use a candle flame as a way to improve your ability to stay centred, enthused and inspired in life.

Of course, a candle flame is a live fire and must be treated with great caution. The World Peace Flame relies on you to use your common sense!

Please read the Appendix, which gives important guidelines for using candles safely.

Health Notes

People with sensitive eyes should not stare directly into a flame.

If you have a mental health condition requiring medication or psychiatric care, your needs are better met by short periods of relaxed focus, rather than by prolonged or deep meditation or relaxation. You can still gain the benefits of the meditations in this book, but think 'little and often', spending only a couple of minutes at a time, two or three times per day. Please ask your medical specialists for further advice.

I would like to add my voice to the chorus of people who realise the critical importance of striving for world peace and who appreciate the symbolic power of the World Peace Flame ... What burns in the hearts of people throughout the world will have expression in the Flames of Peace. Congratulations to all who envisaged this project and who made it happen. Future generations will take comfort and inspiration from you.

Bishop, California
founder, interfaith organisation

PART 1

IGNITING THE FIRE

THE ORIGIN OF THE
WORLD PEACE FLAME

" *My dream is for every man, woman and child in
every nation and country and from every
religion and creed to be united by
the World Peace Flame.* "

Mansukh Patel

THE CALL OF LIGHT

ॐ Birth of an Idea

THE JOURNEYS OF THE FLAMES

ॐ Europe—The Royal Flame of Europe

ॐ Africa—On the First Day

ॐ America—'America the Beautiful'

ॐ Canada—Bridging Three Nations

ॐ Australia—The Spirit Has Landed

ॐ India—From Mahatma Gandhi

ॐ Middle East—The Seventh Light

JOINING THE FLAMES

ॐ Birth of the World Peace Flame

---

*" It was a great pleasure to meet... the World Peace Flame
and to have it in this centre of decision making. "*

Parliamentary Leader, European Parliament
on receiving the World Peace Flame in Brussels

THE CALL OF LIGHT

BIRTH OF AN IDEA

" Someday, after we have mastered the winds, the waves, the tides and gravity… we shall harness the energies of love. Then, for the second time in the history of the world, humanity will have discovered fire. "

Pierre Teilhard de Chardin
1881—1955

The Origin of the
World Peace Flame

H ave you ever experienced a time in your life when you were ready to take a quantum leap forward? You felt like walking out of the old ways of doing things and trying something larger and completely new. All you needed was the right idea.

Just imagine that this idea has entered your mind. You are struck by its perfection but are completely unaware of how far-reaching it will become.

This is how Edison must have felt when he first had the idea for the light bulb — or Mother Teresa when she first thought of going to the streets of Calcutta. How would Gandhi have felt when he first thought of his great Salt March?

History is full of extraordinary turning points that arose from ordinary circumstances. Gandhi's idea of walking to Dandi beach and making salt seemed of little importance at first. 'What use is making salt?' Nehru had asked. 'We'd do better to march to the Viceroy's palace or Downing Street.' Yet Gandhi's Salt March opened the eyes of the whole world to India's plight. It is said to have marked the beginning of the end for the British Empire.

What are the principles that might help us prepare the ground so that we, too, can have far-reaching ideas that will improve the rest of our lives? What can we do to turn these ideas into reality?

Whether we want to take a new step that will dramatically improve the lives of our family or our colleagues, or whether we are looking for a way to stand up and make an ever-remembered contribution to humanity, these principles are the same.

We can learn them by following the examples of others.

Seemingly ordinary men and women through the centuries have taken hold of an extraordinary idea and with it completely altered their lives—and sometimes the very course of history.

This first section of *The Flame that Transforms* brings you the story of one such dramatic turning point. It is the story of an idea that occurred to a group of people and has since gone on to change thousands, perhaps millions, of people's lives.

It will show you how you can create the fertile soil for making your own life a magnificent and exciting adventure.

Welcome to the story of the World Peace Flame.

A Legacy of Fertile Ground

Savitri

There is a seed potential lying dormant in everyone. The World Peace Flame has helped many, many people realise their hopes and aspirations.

For me it was itself the realisation of one of my highest dreams. A flame is all-pervasive; it shines equally on everyone and in all directions, without judgement or condemnation. It also creates friendship and hope. These are the qualities I hold most dear to my heart, qualities which are the legacy of my father.

****   ****   ****

My father had been a prisoner of war in the Dachau concentration camp during the Second World War. As a child on a remote farm on the west coast of Scotland, I often saw him lost in the past, alone and unreachable behind barriers as tangible as the ancient stone walls that surrounded our fields.

As we were growing up, my father always took particular delight in welcoming German pilgrims into our house. Our farm was very close to the route to Iona, Scotland's famous holy island, and pilgrims often stopped at our house to ask for directions. I guess as children we never thought his obvious warmth for Germans was strange as it was perfectly normal for him to insist they came in for tea and a friendly chat.

Then one day, my elder brother came home from school to find our house once again full of German visitors, all sitting with my father, laughing and joking.

This time was different though. My brother had just been attending European history classes and—in the biased history of the day—had been learning exactly who the good and bad guys had been. He stood there, overwhelmed by fury. As soon as he could, he grabbed my father and yelled, 'How can you do this? How can you sit in the same room with these people and feed them after what they did to you!?'

Not surprisingly the visitors soon left. My father called all of us children together by the fireside and we sat around him in nervous anticipation, expecting a huge telling off. However, instead, his eyes grew soft and he looked at each of us in turn. Then, for the first time ever, he began to tell us about his experiences in the concentration camp. His words completely changed my life.

'During the day,' he said, his voice filling with memories, 'the soldiers used to take us out to work in the fields. Then, once we got there, they would stand aside and smoke cigarettes, leaving us under the direction of the local farmers.'

He paused, waiting for our reaction. The four of us sat spellbound, glued to his words—we'd never heard what happened to him in the camps, even though his time there was quietly spoken about every now and then.

'Once in a while,' he continued, 'one of the farmers would rush up to us with a big stick, yelling and shouting, 'Work harder!' The farmer would raise the stick high to hit us and then in a very low voice say, 'I've put some bread for you in that haystack over there.' He'd then pretend to beat us, hitting us as lightly as he could. Sometimes, that bread was all we had to eat for the whole day. At other times, the farmers would start a commotion by shouting and throwing large stones at us. When they landed, we found they weren't stones at all. They were pieces of bread.

'If it were not for those German people,' my father said, 'I would not be alive today—and neither would you. Those farmers risked their lives to save mine. Please,' he implored, 'never, ever judge or condemn a nation because of the actions of a few.'

That statement went straight into my heart. I was overwhelmed by the contrast between my father's complete lack of hatred and the terrors he had endured. In moments like these I believe a human being has the power to reach into the highest parts of another person's soul and evoke a strength that will stay with them for a lifetime. From that day forward I found I no longer had it in me to pre-judge anyone. It was one of the greatest lessons of my life.

Not long after that, my nine-year-old world turned upside down.

My father had just returned from the nearest town on farm business. It was a long journey, so he had stayed overnight with a friend who happened to have a large collection of guns.

The next day two policemen came to our door. A gun had been stolen from the collection and my father, along with two others, was suspected of the theft. He received a harsh letter from his friend's lawyers, followed by a further phone call from the police.

Something in him must have snapped. Their judgement and condemnation cut too close to the traumas he had been through.

That night he took his own gun, went out and shot himself.

I ran away to the mountains and cried solidly for five or six hours. My grief was too great to share with anyone, even my mother. But nature has its own protection for a child, and as I lay on the ground sobbing, a shocked numbness began to settle around my heart, providing a buffer from the storm of emotions.

After a while I picked myself up and returned home. The rest of my family continued their grieving process, but I acted as if nothing had happened. Even though my mother tried to help me, I just couldn't find the healing I needed. I didn't know how to express the wild questioning that raged in my heart.

Why did my father die? Two days later we received a letter saying the gun had been found, and apologising for 'any inconvenience'. I just couldn't believe it. *Why did he have to die?* He had been the kindest and most accepting man I could imagine. He had done everything to instil those same qualities in us and now he was gone. Gone forever because of people's suspicion and a stupid misunderstanding. Why did it have to happen like this? It was too much for me to bear.

When the light of your life disappears forever, the loss is so great you are driven to do one of three things: to escape, close down completely or make a journey of discovery.

By some grace, my young mind chose the path of discovery. Light has a way of calling you, attracting you irresistibly towards its source.

The questions never went away, but as time went on I began to find some answers. My father's positive attributes had become part of me, too, part of the very fabric of my soul. As I grew older I found myself unwilling to criticise or condemn others and I began to travel the world trying to earn my living with the same integrity I remembered in my father. As each year taught me new ways to help others, I experienced more and more healing within myself. Eventually I encountered the Life Foundation and its way of combining professional humanitarian assistance with a solid core of spirituality. Most importantly, I met Mansukh's parents, Chhaganbhai and Ecchaben Patel, who had worked with Mahatma Gandhi in India.

Mansukh's father, Chhaganbhai, was fourteen years old when he first heard of Gandhi. At that young age he was already a foreman in a textile mill, responsible for some 300 young people who worked under him. He was inspired by Gandhi's method of non-violence and campaigned for better working conditions, organising the first non-violent strike in the mill. At the age of seventeen he met Gandhi himself and remained a committed Gandhian for the rest of his life.

It was under Chhaganbhai's guidance that I first learned how a small body of people can work together with such unity, tolerance and joy that their very teamwork becomes a source of nourishment and strength.

Above all, Mansukh's parents taught me how to use the light of a flame to heal the pain of my past. They showed me how it can awaken the longing to know who you are and align yourself to the simple truth that the moment in front of you is all you have.

Over the years, with my colleagues in the Life Foundation, I began to take these methods out to heal others. In conflict zones such as Northern Ireland, Bosnia or the North Caucasus I learned how a flame can give tremendous hope and bring you into harmony with those around you. I discovered how sharing a flame with another human being can take away the feeling of helplessness and hopelessness.

I worked with people from all stations of life and found that no matter who you are, a flame has the power to bring you back to a point of believing in yourself, in life and in nature.

Gradually, as our work took us to some of the most challenging places in the world, I became aware that immense reserves of energy were building up within me.

My father's legacy had prepared the ground inside me well.

****   ****   ****

By the first few months of 1999 my colleagues in the Life Foundation and I could all feel that we were ready for a bold new step forward. We had been gathering skills and experience, teaching people in most of the major cultures of the world and had begun working in war zones, helping people heal emotional trauma. We had seen the aftermath of violence and knew the value of peace. Like many people before us, we wanted to step up our contribution to the world.

The Millennium was approaching and we were eager to take on a truly global initiative. For many months we had all, individually and in small groups, been thinking about what we could do.

All we needed now was the idea.

Ignition ~ The Birth of an Idea

Mansukh

Growing up in Kenya's Rift Valley in the aftermath of the Mau Mau civil war painted the reality of suffering indelibly on my soul. Although the political war had ended before I was born, the atrocities committed by the warring communities continued well into the sixties. There were times when entire Asian families were being systematically murdered near our home.

When trauma and pain arise in our lives we need someone who can be a guide and give us some form of shelter. My parents, through all they had learned from Mahatma Gandhi, taught me how to rise up from the ashes of devastation and go on to create a new and more vital life.

They carried their secret so naturally that for many years I was hardly aware of its power. Eventually I realised that not everyone's parents had the same interpersonal skills and humble courage as mine. Gradually, they began to teach me and a small group of friends from university everything they knew.

If I were to sum up their wisdom in one simple sentence it would be this: the happiness you experience is directly proportional to the degree to which you live to bring happiness to others.

For more than twenty years my friends and I have endeavoured to create a lifestyle that expresses this truth.

By the first few months of 1999, only eight months from the turn of the Millennium, we were looking for a way to offer this collected experience out to the world on a global scale.

**** **** ****

When you are searching for a cherished goal it often won't appear until you let go of the effort of trying to find it. Letting go is paramount. It allows the space for providence to enter your life and help you out.

Still, the *preparation* you put into your search is all important. My father always said, 'Success occurs when preparation meets opportunity.'

In our case, these two great forces converged when a small group of us answered a call for help.

A few years previously my sister, Pushpaben, had lost her husband. Now a middle-aged woman, she had no-one to help her maintain her house in Bolton, Lancashire, nor could she afford to pay someone to help her.

So early in April 1999, Savitri, myself and four other colleagues travelled to the North of England and met at Pushpaben's house for a 'decorating holiday'. For three days we transformed the house, laughing together, eating together, painting walls, ceilings, cupboards and even each other in our enjoyment at spending a holiday helping someone in need.

At the end of our final day together we sat and reminisced about our teaching experiences in so many different parts of the world. Pushpaben's house happened to be in the same area as the cotton mills that Gandhi visited in the 1930s and we wondered how he must have felt as he walked these streets. What did he think, what did he say, what did he do?

Pushpaben got up and began to cook a traditional family meal for us, singing an old song of my mother's as she moved around the dimly lit kitchen. Rita Goswami began to sing with her. Suddenly Pushpaben's presence, so very like my mother's, combined with the smells of the food to take me straight back to my childhood in Africa. I felt I was in two places at once—the hard soil of Africa and a terraced house in England.

With this feeling came an intense gratitude for the people in the room who had been working with me for so long. Pushpaben had carried me on her back for years when I was a young child. Rita had been with John Jones, Chris Barrington and me when we set up the Life Foundation nearly twenty years earlier. Lalita Doerstel had transformed the effects of post-war traumas in Germany into a tremendous power for peace and helped John and myself in our first tour of the Continent.

Suddenly, my gratitude and all the memories of my childhood combined into an overwhelming awareness of the legacy of my parents.

'I want to tell you something I have never shared before,' I found myself saying.

'One day, when I was quite young and still living in Kenya, my parents took me to visit a family in an outlying homestead.

'We had no idea what we would encounter when we got there. We didn't know that the Mau Mau guerrillas had raided the place during the night. They had killed everybody—mothers, fathers, children. Not even the animals had been left alive.

'It was one of the most difficult days of my life. We all helped tend to the dead and eventually arrived home at dusk. As soon as she was in the door, my mother went across the room and lit our family diva[1].

'My father stayed outside and sat in silent vigil throughout the night. I fell asleep in the main room next to my mother and I remember waking several times to see her still tending the flame and quietly praying.

'I'll never forget that soft golden light flickering in the dark. Gradually, a soothing mantle of peace settled over my mind.

'Whenever you are tired, ill, or overcome with sadness, Mansukh,' my mother said, 'light a flame. It will bring healing

---

[1] A diva is a small butter-lamp. It is made from a brass or copper dish containing a flame burning on a hand-made cotton wick.

to your soul and peace to your mind.'

'Every time the war came close to our village, one of my parents would light that flame. Every time! They taught me how to respond to suffering without adding to the sadness around me.

'In the Bible Jesus tells us about the light. He reminds us not to hide it under a bushel but rather to let it shine for all to see. My parents' light was just like that. It reminded me of who I was, and made me feel as if nothing could hurt my innermost heart.'

I looked around the room. Savitri and the others were spellbound, listening in the semi-darkness.

'Many years later, when I began university, my parents came with me to see my new room. As my mother and I sat on the bed, my father gave me a package, carefully wrapped in red cloth. Inside the cloth, polished and gleaming, was our family diva.

'I carefully lit the diva while my father watched me, eyes glittering with excitement. 'It is time,' he said. 'This has been in our family for generations, as you know, Mansukh. Now it is time for you to carry on the tradition.

'It is the nature of a flame of peace that people will always gather around it,' he said. 'This diva has been a source of inspiration for generations and it will undoubtedly continue to be so for you and your friends. It will be a willing companion for you to dialogue with, although it may take many years before you fully understand its potential.'

'My father continued, describing how the power of this flame would keep gathering momentum. 'It will offer solace to your heart at times of conflict and doubt,' he said. 'And as sure as the sun rises in the morning and the moon follows across the sky at night, you and your friends will rise to embrace its gifts.'

'I was aware of a power that had entered the room at my father's words. 'What do I have to do to make this happen?' I asked.

'He responded, smiling. 'Just light it.'

'Light it every day, Mansukh,' whispered my mother. And that was all the instruction they would give.'

I turned to my friends in Pushpaben's living room.

'So far everything my father has said has come true. I don't know what's to come next, but I've learnt by experience to have implicit faith in his words. Do you remember how we asked thousands of people on our walk from Auschwitz to North Wales to light a candle for peace at a specific time on a specific day? Together we created a river of light across Europe. There is no doubt in my heart that the light he and my mother passed to me that day has prepared the ground for something that will one day reverberate through the portals of history.'

It was exactly the catalyst we had been waiting for.

'Mansukh,' Savitri began in excitement, 'I've been thinking about the way the Olympic Flame is carried from one continent to another... What if we got flames for peace lit on each continent...?'

In a flash, someone else caught it. 'Yes! We could get them all brought to the UK...'

Suddenly the idea we had been searching for was with us! We were off, each new idea building upon the previous with such supercharged energy that they felt like flashes of lightning across the sky. 'Flames of Peace... lit on each continent... flown across the oceans to the UK... combined together... one Flame of Peace uniting every person of the world... people could take flames lit from this one back to their own homes...'

Realisation flooded me. *This was it!* This was exactly what Mum and Dad were talking about all those years ago! Tears of gratitude filled my eyes. I felt we had finally assumed the mantle of my parents.

Late into the night we discussed the idea, captured by the excitement of what the Flames of Peace would mean for each other and for the world. We were like children who had discovered a long-hidden treasure. We felt we were envisaging something that had already become a reality.

**** **** ****

By the early hours of the morning the idea for the Flames of Peace project had gained shape and form.

We would create a World Peace Flame to greet the dawn of the new Millennium.

We would light Flames of Peace on the world's continents and fly them all, Olympic style, to the UK. Each Flame would carry that continent's hopes for liberty, justice, peace and freedom.

We would then unite them to produce a single flame, the World Peace Flame, which would represent the entire world.

People could take lights from this new World Peace Flame, and use them as a reminder of their potential to contribute to the world.

Nothing on this scale had ever been achieved before. The idea had the potential to help thousands, perhaps millions of people reach a new level of awareness and inner strength. In time it could come to represent the aspirations for peace of all humanity.

We fixed a date and time for the uniting of the Flames: Saturday, 31st July, at our International Life Conference in North Wales, UK.

It was early April.

We had just three and a half months to make it all happen.

The sole meaning of life is to serve humanity.
Leo Tolstoy

THE ROYAL FLAME OF EUROPE

THE JOURNEY OF THE FIRST FLAME

" When you are inspired by some great purpose, some extraordinary project, all your thoughts break their bonds.

Your mind transcends limitations, expands in every direction and you find yourself in a new, great and wonderful world.

Dormant forces, faculties and talents become alive and you discover yourself to be a greater person by far than you ever dreamed yourself to be. "

Patanjali
c. 500 B.C.

The First Lighting

Savitri

The sky was as black as I had ever seen it as I made my way through torrential rain to the home of Irene van Lippe Biesterfeld, Princess of The Netherlands. It was 20th June, 1999, two and a half months after our first meeting in Lancashire at Pushpaben's house.

I had called Irene a few weeks earlier and asked if she would consent to light the European Flame of Peace. She had made it her life's work to inspire people to discover their inner strengths and I was sure she was the right person to light the Flame. Consequently, I carefully held this certainty foremost in my mind as we talked. She is an extremely busy woman, managing a successful career as an author and workshop facilitator as well as a host of other responsibilities. What would she say?

I think the magnitude of our vision touched her. After a few moments of thought she said yes, and invited us to hold a flame lighting ceremony at her own residence.

The wild and stormy weather did not let up for a moment during our drive. Thunder rolled constantly from huge black clouds and occasional forks of lightning struck the horizon. Why, I mused, were conditions so dreadful on the very day we had chosen to light the first Flame of Peace?

We arrived outside Irene's house and hurried out of the car into the congenial atmosphere of her workshop room. She had two colleagues with her and I was met by my co-workers, Nanna, Trudy and Theodore.

Irene and I had already discussed the form of the ceremony

and she had carefully arranged the room beforehand. Everything was ready for us to begin.

Two months of intense preparation were about to come to a single point of focus. When you begin a new initiative, its power builds fastest when you take at least one positive action towards it every day. Ever since our meeting in Lancashire we had personally followed this principle, and by now our collective daily outpouring had created an immense momentum. The first of the Flames of Peace was about to be born!

We began in silence and I led a short contemplation, asking everyone to focus intently on every person in Europe. Could we, I asked, draw upon their love and yearning for peace? I held in my heart a prayer that this Flame would become a great carrier of light, a great healer of nations.

As I spoke I sensed our unity of purpose. Nanna began to play an ancient song of peace on her flute, while Irene struck a match and gently touched it to the wick on the lantern. I carefully replaced its glass and sat back.

So deep was the ensuing silence that we all closed our eyes and fell into a timeless space of utter peace. We felt captivated by a force greater than ourselves, lost in wonder.

And then I opened my eyes to see Irene looking at me with delight. The Flame flickered merrily in the lamp and a look of sheer joy passed between us. The European Flame of Peace had been born!

Suddenly there was a break in the clouds and the room filled with light. We hadn't seen the sun all day but somehow, impossibly, it burst out of the darkness, flooding us with bright, watery, crystal clear light. The window frame had two cross-pieces that cast a perfectly formed shadow of a cross. We gasped in amazement.

Our lamp lay precisely at the centre of the two arms of the cross. We were speechless, marvelling at the sight before us.

Irene grasped the power of the moment. Quietly remarking that the Flame obviously had immense healing power, she asked us to pray that its first action would be to bring healing to a close friend who had been so ill he had lost his will to live.

The ceremony now complete, we departed, carrying the vast creative presence of the newly born Flame of Peace back to our centre in the east of The Netherlands.

Two days later I received news from Irene that her friend had 'suddenly' regained his will to live, and that his vigour and enthusiasm for life were now returning. Had our Flame contributed to his recovery, I wondered? A magical feeling of infinite possibilities was beginning to envelop our work.

Now, we had to fly the Flame to the UK.

The Quest to Fly the Flames

Savitri

How do you find someone who will carry a live flame across the oceans to another continent? Right from the start it was clear that we would have to fly the Flames of Peace, as there simply wasn't enough time to arrange for surface transport. How then could we arrange for them to fly?

Our project had never been accomplished before, but there were precedents. The Olympic Flame is flown from one continent to another so surely, we felt, our goal must be possible.

We began the job of contacting airlines from our office in The Netherlands. As we began to find our way through airline offices around the world, a common pattern emerged. Qantas, the Australian airline, typified the response.

'I like your idea,' the Public Relations Officer said during our first conversation with him. 'We've carried elephants, live alligators and the entire Grand Prix. I'm sure a tiny flame in a safety lamp won't be any problem at all.

'I'll just check with our safety people and get back to you.'

A few days later, he was not so optimistic.

'Well,' he said, 'it appears that in order to fly the Olympic Flame we have to get permission from every country along the flight path before we can carry a naked flame over their territory. Not only that, there is a rule in our international airline agreement that specifically forbids naked flames in flight. It would take us years to get over all this red tape, and you're trying to do it all in a few weeks.

'I'm sorry,' he concluded. 'I think what you're trying to do is impossible.'

History is full of great triumphs built on successions of apparent failures. Soon we were calling the head offices of airlines across the world, some of the team working through the night because of time differences, and sleeping during the day.

Nevertheless, as we neared the end of June, only a month from the date we'd planned to bring all the Flames together, we were still drawing a blank. What could we do?

The breakthrough finally came while I was away in Norway, teaching techniques for healing emotional trauma to a group of child psychologists from Chechnya.

There are times in your life when you face an ultimate crisis, when you have given everything you feel capable of, and yet you find that still more is required. The crisis forces you to look for a strength that lies far beyond your own personal ability.

On the second day of the programme, I had to search for strength as I had never searched before.

When I had joined the Chechen group, they had already undergone a variety of re-enactment therapies. That morning, they had focused on the experience of one of the women in the group.

During the war in Chechnya the woman, along with her brother and many of the people in our training group, had been sitting in a café when the door was thrust open and a live grenade thrown into the room. People screamed and fell over each other trying to get away—everyone except the woman's brother. He had dived towards the grenade, pressed it to his stomach and doubled over to protect everyone else from the blast. He sacrificed his life to save everyone else.

Re-enacting this scene had taken these brave people back into a severe trauma. By the end of the day I had only just managed to help them clear some of the worst rawness of their pain and the effort had left me deeply tired.

Then I received a call from Nanna Coppens, our office co-ordinator in The Netherlands.

The rest of the team were beginning to think they had exhausted all the options for flying the Flames to the UK. Nanna brightly suggested an alternative. 'We could get the Flame shipped over,' she said, 'or transported by road…' Her voice trailed away in the face of my silence. We both knew there was no way the Flames would all arrive on time unless they were flown.

When you know that something is meant to happen, and devote all your energy to making sure you achieve it, amazing faculties awaken within you. I have found that one of these faculties is an inner knowing that acts like a pilot, constantly telling you which direction to take.

As Nanna spoke, this inner knowing erupted inside me.

'Nanna, please,' I begged, 'you and the team *can* do it.' My voice was calm, but intense with passion. 'There is someone out there who is waiting to fly these Flames, I know. *Please* don't give up on these flights so soon!'

It only takes a moment to waver off your course. In my experience, as soon as you opt for an easier path—even for an instant—you sabotage your commitment to your original goal. And then it just fades away before your eyes.

That night, I sat alone in my room. Here I had a group of highly traumatised people around me, desperate for help, while in The Netherlands the team were doing everything they could, yet still not finding a solution.

We had reached the limits of what we knew. Now we needed help.

A long time ago, Mansukh's father had taught me a meditation technique that involved sitting by a flame for several hours. When you open yourself to its light, it awakens your awareness to your own higher potential.

All that night, I sat up alone in my room with my flame, searching for answers in our seemingly impossible situation.

Halfway through the next day, Nanna called back.

She and Quirine Wentink, one of our key team members in The Netherlands, had been going over every possible avenue for flying the Flames. They had reached a point where they were open to any idea, no matter how wild.

Suddenly, there it was. Quirine had a flash of inspiration. 'Hey,' she said, 'why don't we try the air forces? They might help us.'

They called Trudy de Ruyter, our public liaison officer, who immediately went into action. After many calls she was finally referred to a man named Colonel Harts. His name, to her, summed up our work. She sensed it was a good beginning.

Over in Norway, halfway through my afternoon training session, I was called away from the group to take an urgent telephone call. It was Nanna, who could barely contain her excitement. Colonel Harts had said yes! His approval was conditional on a further meeting, but things looked very hopeful indeed. 'Wait till you hear this though,' Nanna continued. 'The most likely date for the flight will be next Wednesday. That's 7th July, your fortieth birthday!'

I was in a daze as I returned to my group of refugees. I had also had an extraordinary day. From early that morning I had been to visit each of the most badly traumatised women, personally massaging their hands, feet and faces, helping them feel the healing power of friendship. I had then given talks with fascinating new ideas, entertained them with humour and taken them outside for gentle movement therapy. Together we had cleared away much of their earlier trauma.

By the time Nanna phoned I knew I had made tremendous progress. Her call on top of this was like a magnificent completion. If yesterday had been one of the most challenging days of my life, today had become one of my most triumphant.

Had that late night meditation been responsible for this? What had opened our minds to the ideas that had made our day flow so perfectly? I was in awe at the simple possibility that such power had been liberated by the light of a flame.

We had built an unshakeable foundation against apparently insurmountable odds. Now we were ready to face one final test.

When the Life Foundation contacted us to ask for help with transporting the Peace Flames, our first thought was of the air force restrictions that apply to carrying naked flames on board an aircraft. But we only hesitated for a moment. As soon as the purpose of the project was explained to us, we immediately understood its unique symbolic nature and did everything we could to make it possible. It has been an incredible success.

Our involvement in the Peace Flame Operation has made me reflect deeply about the work of the Life Foundation and also about peace itself. After we had completed the project I was posted to Ethiopia, following the war with Eritrea. That certainly makes you think about how you can find different ways of establishing peace in the world. I very much appreciate the methods used by the Life Foundation. Without taking sides themselves, they work to open a dialogue between the conflicting parties to try to bring the two sides together.

I hope that in the future we will be able to fly with materials other than bombs, and that we will be able to help humanity work towards peace in a different way. This is something we have already partly established, for example by flying refugees out of Kosovo.

May the World Peace Flame lead to a world in which air forces only deliver aid and not force.

Colonel J. M. Harts
Royal Netherlands Air Force

It was about making a 'mission impossible' possible. When I first heard of the idea of transporting the Flames, and the apparent contradiction of an air force—a military organisation—working with a peace initiative from the Life Foundation, I thought it was a good opportunity not to refuse to look at alternative ways of doing things.

Once we had completed our mission to fly the Flame to Birmingham, it seemed that everyone knew about the project. Suddenly I received a call from an officer at Sri Lankan Airlines, wanting to know all the details of how we had transported the lamp. A little while later the British Royal Air Force asked the same question, and the South African Air Force also arrived at our office by fax and telephone. So, from one moment to the next I had new acquaintances in far away countries.

You know the result. The lamps all eventually arrived in Britain.

Major P. de Ruyter
Royal Netherlands Air Force

Arrival

Savitri

On Monday, 5th July, Trudy and I met with the relevant authorities at the Royal Netherlands Air Force base at Eindhoven, in the south of the country. We were greeted warmly by the officer responsible for operational safety, Major Peter de Ruyter, and several others.

I presented the idea of the Flames of Peace to them, trying to convey the heart and soul behind the project. As I did so, I could feel a deep understanding arising between us. And with this understanding, agreement was soon reached.

In the warmth following the meeting I turned to Major de Ruyter. 'I don't suppose you have contacts in any of the other air forces who might help?' I asked. I gave him a list of the countries we were thinking of bringing Flames from.

He grinned. 'Well, it just so happens we have a flight ourselves coming over from Canada on Thursday. Get your Flame to Winnipeg airport, and we'll do the rest.'

It was the beginning of an alliance between a peace group and an air force that was to create a profoundly symbolic initiative of peace.

For the next 36 hours, Major de Ruyter devoted enormous effort to designing and constructing a flame-proof box which would enable the plane carrying our Flame to meet all the necessary safety regulations. Eventually, his design was able to protect the lamps from every possible mishap.

On 7th July, Colonel Harts and Major de Ruyter joined me at Eindhoven airport. Nearly one hundred of our closest friends in The Netherlands came to see us off and our youth group put on a splendid impromptu performance in the airport lobby.

We had done it. Now that one Flame was on its way, we knew it would be possible to fly the others. The date we planned to unite the Flames was twenty-four days away and we were ready to begin our race to completion.

As I paused to wave goodbye at the doorway into the aircraft, the European Flame glowing brightly beside me, I felt enveloped by a force that was completely larger than life. I felt invincible, radiant, as if I extended twenty feet in every direction. I felt sure that if someone had sent a dart towards me it would have stopped fifteen feet away.

At the other end of our journey, Mansukh, the rest of our team, and the Lord Mayor of Birmingham were waiting for us at Arrivals with a brass band and an official welcome.

Yet, I was hardly present within the formality of the speeches, the media interviews and the flashing cameras.

All I could think of was that the first Flame of Peace had arrived safely in Britain.

ON THE FIRST DAY

THE JOURNEY OF THE AFRICAN FLAME

*" Let there be justice for all. Let there be peace for all.
Let there be work, bread, water and salt for all.
Let each know that for each the body,
the mind and the soul have been
freed to fulfil themselves. "*

Nelson Mandela

Encounter at the Border

Mansukh

My father often told me, 'When an idea from the great collective consciousness of humanity captures you, never hesitate for a moment until it has been fulfilled.' And certainly, by the time we left Lancashire to return to our home base in North Wales, the Peace Flames project had grown into something far greater than 'our idea'. It was like a gift that had been handed to us, fully formed and alive. Every part of my mind was turning over its possibilities. I was eager to see it begin.

Consequently, the first thing I did when I got home was to meet with Julie Hotchkiss, the co-ordinator of our international outreach centres. Julie is the kind of person who embraces a new project as if it has already been completed, so right from the start she insisted we follow two key principles in our work on the Flames. Firstly, we decided only to add to each other's ideas and, secondly, we began to speak about the project as if it had already been completed. Her advice brought us astounding results, and we began to watch our ideas falling into place like pieces of a jigsaw. Soon she and her team were busy with the manifold details of this vast project, while my own role involved going back to Africa, the land of my birth.

Over the previous six months we had already been scheduling a series of trainings and seminars in South Africa and Kenya. I had been planning to travel to South Africa with Paulette Agnew, co-ordinator of our African projects, while Andrew had been organising parallel trainings in Kenya along with Anita Goswami, another of our senior detraumatisation trainers. We'd planned to meet again by mid-June in Northern Kenya and then make a brief journey together into the vast beauty of the Rift Valley, where I was born. It would be my first visit back there in thirty-five years.

Each of us involved in lighting the Flames was eating, breathing and sleeping the project, trying to make a dream come alive not just for ourselves but for a world of people we may never meet. Martin Luther King once said, 'The important question is *What can I do for others?*' We were discovering the truth of his words, and an even greater principle beyond. The constant 'co-incidences' and miracles of timing we were beginning to experience couldn't have been happening if just one of us had been working alone. Our personal friendships with each other and the bridges being created by our innumerable telephone calls around the world seemed to be liberating a force that appeared capable of achieving anything.

Soon we were to put this principle to the test with our very lives.

Around the time Savitri was lighting the European Flame, Paulette and I joined Andrew and Anita in Northern Kenya where the two of them had spent a week training seventy Sudanese refugees and aid workers at the large United Nations base at Lokichokio. Their work had been so successful that we were all invited across the border into war-torn South Sudan to experience for ourselves the conditions of the Sudanese within their homeland. We travelled across the no-man's land in the company of an armed land-cruiser bristling with fifteen men armed with AK-47s. Once in Sudan we were given wonderful hospitality, but then, on our return across the border into Kenya, we encountered the stark reality of war.

Travelling along a dirt road, we reached a rough wooden boom-gate which marked the border. Our documents were checked by the guards and we were given clearance to go ahead. Thankfully we began to move forward, feeling tired yet happy and relieved to be moving on again.

Suddenly, a young soldier barked a command. 'What are you smiling at?!' he snapped, as the boom-gate lowered again, blocking our way. The driver of our land-cruiser stiffened in fear.

'This is an international border,' the guard continued fiercely, 'where you should show respect! Who do you think you are?'

He looked a little drunk, or maybe drugged, and we could only guess at the traumas he must have endured.

Intuitively, each of us searched for ways in which to build a relationship with this young man. He asked us a lot of questions and as we answered him we complimented him on his role in the command post, exchanged names with him and searched for ways we might build a rapport with him about his country. He wasn't impressed.

'Get out of the vehicle,' he said abruptly.

'Don't do it!' whispered our driver, gripping the steering wheel. We sat tight and politely ignored the soldier's request and instead invited him to look through the back of the vehicle at everything we were carrying. He looked capable of anything, and we were beginning to comprehend our precarious situation. It was vital we created a relationship with him. We each put every ounce of our energy and enthusiasm into surrounding him with light and building a bridge of sincere friendship and respect towards him.

Gradually, he began to change. First he laughed in response to one of our attempts at humour. Then, our politeness began to give him the assurance he needed, and eventually he favoured us with a genuine smile. Finally, he was satisfied.

'Okay, you can go.' The boom swung up and we thanked him as our vehicle moved off.

It was only later that the reality of our danger really came home to us. For a few moments then our lives had hung on a thread. Our earnest attempt to establish a connection of light and friendship with that young man may have actually saved our lives. As the only foreigners for miles around, our disappearance could have gone unnoticed for days.

Even though some of us were shaken by the trauma of the incident, at the same time we were jubilant. Because our whole project with the Flames was so important to us, it was inevitable that a major challenge would come our way. That is the way of life. Now that challenge had been firmly met and overcome we had no doubt that doorways would already be opening ahead of us, leading us into the next stage of our work.

Home to the Cradle of Humanity

Mansukh

If our desire to create friendship and empathy with a trau-matised soldier at a remote border crossing could save lives, what could these principles do if all of humanity were to apply them? This thought was uppermost in my mind a few days later as we drove towards my childhood home in the Rift Valley.

We were driving into the area often referred to as the Cradle of Humanity. Two million years ago, our earliest ancestors walked this very soil. It must have been here that they first dis-covered fire. Now we had come back to this land to ignite a second kind of fire, the fire of friendship and unity.

It was the perfect place to kindle the spontaneous, uninhib-ited power of the Flame of Peace for Africa.

I was so moved to be re-entering this land after being away such a long time that I could hardly speak.

By one of those quirks of co-incidence our dates had 'just happened' to work out perfectly. Today was my forty-fourth birthday. In our work we constantly look for opportunities to create 'magical moments' for each other, and Andrew and Anita had been unable to resist the opportunity. Unbeknown to me, they had come here two weeks previously and organ-ised a complete itinerary around the most special places I remembered from my childhood. It was one of the best birth-day presents I had ever received.

Gilgil, the little town where I was born, lies sixty-five kilo-metres north east of Nairobi. As we drove towards it in the pre-dawn half-light I saw herds of zebras and giraffes roaming freely and Maasai tribes-people still living in their traditional way. The wide, brown plains stretched away into a soft, end-less heat haze, dotted occasionally with immense acacia trees standing like timeless sentinels.

Returning to your childhood home after so long gives you a completely new perspective on yourself. All the earliest and greatest lessons of your life stand out in clear relief.

Here, by this low ridge, I had run for my life from a lioness and afterwards my father had taught me how to use my breathing to overcome my fear. There was the patch of road where I had witnessed the death of a boyhood friend, and my mother had first shown me how to use a flame to heal the deep, deep pain it had created. Above us was the mountain where I used to sit before dawn in silent meditation with my father. He had taught me there about the forces that become available to you when you sit in profound silence outside in nature.

Overwhelmed by these memories, I found myself letting go of the intricate details of my normal adult life—all those details which can be so unnecessarily preoccupying. I felt a wonder-ful release from burdens I hadn't even noticed I was carrying.

We reached the foot of the mountain, halted the car and began to climb. Half way to the top, the dawn shot brilliant rays of gold all around us. I thought of everyone working so hard on the Flame project back home and readied myself to light the African Flame. But where should we light it? On the top of this mountain? Or down below in the village amidst all the people?

We reached the summit and sat down. Soon we found our-selves immersed in silence.

I remembered how, one day when I was nine, I had climbed into a car with no-one but my family and nothing but the clothes I stood up in. I hadn't known I was leaving the area for good. Now, thirty-five years later, I had returned here with nothing (courtesy of my airline, which had lost all my luggage en route) and no-one other than some of my dearest friends.

With this thought I looked up through the rays of the sun and there, above us, was a magnificent eagle.

In our tradition the eagle is revered as the herald of a great truth. Gazing at it, I realised that I had completed one immense revolution in the spiral of life.

On the slopes of this mountain, my father had guided me into the deepest meditation and shown me how our outward journey through life must be balanced with the inward journey towards our soul. I remembered his words about our flame of peace in my university bedroom all those years before: 'You and your friends will rise to embrace its gifts.' I checked the sun. It wasn't quite overhead, and I realised that it must be almost the exact time of my birth.

If, today, one cycle of my life had been completed, then surely another was about to begin. I was certain that the Flames of Peace were its beginning.

It was time to go. I knew now that the African Flame should be lit not in solitude, but amidst the friendship and community of the people of this great continent.

A Dream Stronger than the Wind

Mansukh

We descended the mountain and made our way to the house where I was born. Dozens of noisy, exuberant children ran forward to greet us as we entered the huge corrugated iron doors that formed the entrance to the corral in which I grew up. Andrew and Anita had prepared everything well and we were greeted from across the courtyard by Jane Kanuthia, the mother of the family that currently lives in my parents' old house. Smiling in welcome, she invited us in.

Have you ever had the experience of walking into a house you knew intimately many years ago? I was entranced. Every nook and cranny was warmly familiar, yet completely foreign to my adult mind. Within these rooms, in the dim light of our hurricane lamp, my mother had taught me that while everything in life changes over the years, there is a place within us that remains the same through the different stages of our lives. 'Find this place, Mansukh,' she used to say to me. 'Within it lies our greatest strength.' I hoped that our Flames of Peace would one day serve to remind millions of people of this truth.

With this realisation, I knew that this was where the Flame of Africa should be lit.

Jane's husband, Joseph, soon returned home from work. The two of them couldn't believe that people from Europe were sitting in their living room and talking about a project that could help bring peace to the whole world.

As we began our Flame lighting ceremony, Joseph was so

inspired that he led us with unrestrained exuberance into his church's gospel hymns. We all joined in and it began to feel as if all of Africa was with us. Sitting in that tiny living room, black, brown and white hands clasped together, we sang the traditional African songs, the rousing music taking our aware-ness far beyond the walls of the room and out to fill the whole of the African continent. I struck the match and lit the lantern. It seemed to me that the light swelled of its own accord, grow-ing in strength as it crossed plains, touched upon mountains, forests and rivers, and finally found fullness by the shores of the oceans. Africa was a light to the world, and this light had come to rest upon our lamp.

That night I sat outside with the Flame flickering beside me, tiny and still inside its lantern, yet looking so vulnerable. It reminded me how fragile our dreams can be. Anyone could blow it out—if you let them. Yet I knew that this light was fired by a dream stronger than the wind. I thought of my parents' connection with Gandhi, and through him to Tagore, Thoreau and Tolstoy. Generations of peacemakers had worked to create the flame of peace that my parents had carefully nurtured and tended within this very house.

Now the Flame was ready to be carried to Britain. The South African Air Force had agreed to transport it, and Paulette flew on ahead to South Africa to complete all the arrangements.

I flew back to London, connecting straight to Birmingham to meet Savitri. By complete 'coincidence' my ticket had been booked for 7th July, the very day she had flown the European Flame over to the UK!

Two weeks later, Andrew and Paulette welcomed the African Flame at a large Royal Air Force base near Oxford, in the south of England. They brought it straight into the city and there, in one of the UK's great historic seats of learning, the Lord Mayor of Oxford formally welcomed it into the UK.

The African Flame had arrived in Britain.

AMERICA THE BEAUTIFUL

THE JOURNEY OF THE AMERICAN FLAME

> " *O beautiful for halcyon skies,*
> *For amber waves of grain,*
> *For purple mountain majesties*
> *Above the enamelled plain!* "

> *from 'America the Beautiful'*
> *by Katharine Lee Bates*

'... For Purple Mountain Majesties'

Savitri

J ust about every American knows the song 'America the Beautiful', written by Katharine Lee Bates on the summit of Pikes Peak, a friendly, 14,000 foot presence dominating Colorado's central Front Range.

Lalita Doerstel, Director of Life Foundation North America, was based in Colorado Springs and could see Pikes Peak every time she looked out of her window. So when we invited her to organise the lighting of a Flame for America, she turned to the mountains and knew immediately where the ceremony should take place. Colorado Springs is positioned right in the heart of America, and it felt perfect to light the Flame on the summit of one of its most famous mountains.

She and her team wanted to include as many American voices as possible in the lighting of their Flame. So they visited towns along the Rockies from Denver to Pueblo, asking people to write messages of peace either to a family member, a friend or for the world.

'People were very, very touched,' Lalita said later. 'They were often in tears. We gave them cards to write on, and the simple act of writing a 'postcard' to someone they loved seemed to clear years of pent-up emotion. It was as if they suddenly realised how much they really cared for the person they were writing to.' After four weeks the team—Lalita, Ned Hartfiel, Jeannie Katz and Ron and Deb Houseman—had collected more than 2,000 cards.

Walking is one of the best ways to prepare your body, mind and emotions for a decisive moment in your life. So, on 25th June, 1999, Lalita, Ned and team began a two day walk to the summit of Pikes Peak as a preparation for their Flame lighting ceremony. Near the top, the air became so thin that they had to rest after every ten steps. Nevertheless, on 26th June, the day Mansukh was lighting the Flame for Africa, they reached the summit and gasped in wonder at the panoramic view of plains and mountains before them. It was easy to understand why Katharine Lee Bates had penned such magnificent lines and why this is one of America's most visited mountains.

As they prepared to start the lighting ceremony the special train that brings tourists to the summit arrived. The team explained their work to a crowd of curious onlookers, and then spread out to six different locations.

'We read out every one of the messages we had collected,' said Ned afterwards. 'It was a tremendous experience. Initially we weren't sure how we would get on, each of us reading more than 300 cards out loud, but after a while we could almost feel those heartfelt prayers of peace being heard.'

An older woman approached Lalita and stood and listened to her reading the messages.

'Honey, can I read out one of those cards?' she asked suddenly. Smiling, Lalita held the bag out for her. The woman reached into it and pulled one out. Turning to the great expanse of America spread out before them she read:

'May my grandson Joey become a peacemaker.'

She stopped, completely stunned, and looked at Lalita.

'*My* grandson's name is also Joey,' she whispered. 'How can this be possible?'

'It was more than just a coincidence,' Lalita told us later. 'The odds against her finding that particular card were impossible, even if she had known it was there. She knew, and I knew, that for some reason we couldn't comprehend, she'd come to the top of Pikes Peak that day especially to offer that message of peace for her grandson.'

It is said that a positive thought never dies in this universe. It echoes outward forever, leaving a trail of creativity in its wake. Lalita and the woman looked at each other, feeling certain that a unique gift had just been sent to that young boy's life.

When they finished reading their cards, each of the team converged back to where their special safety lantern had been prepared. Below them, and slightly to the south, they could see Cheyenne Mountain, bristling with strange antennae. It is the command centre for NORAD, vital to America's nuclear capacity. Normally, when seen from the cities far below, it dominates the view nearly as much as Pikes Peak. From high above, however, it featured very small in comparison to the rest of the landscape. Building peace is like that, they felt. Above and beyond all the preparations for war lies an immense, uncharted potential for building friendship and co-operative solutions. All you have to do is lift your perspective.

In this spirit, Lalita and team prepared to light the lantern. Thinking of all their messages of peace, they let their minds roam outwards, acknowledging all the prayers for justice and liberty across the country—prayers that their eyes would never read, their ears would never hear. Then Lalita touched a match to the wick.

Filled with creativity and imaginative power, the American Flame flared up and danced brightly in the centre of America.

It was now ready to be taken across the ocean to Britain.

Letter addressed to Lalita Doerstel from the Mayor of Colorado Springs, on the occasion of the lighting of the American Flame of Peace:

Organizations like yours are an invaluable spiritual resource to the entire world.

As a citizen and as Mayor, I am deeply moved that our community and its magnificent mountain was selected as the North American site for the June ascent and vigil atop Pikes Peak. I am certain that it was a very moving experience for anyone fortunate enough to be there.

Imagine the impact of those many prayers… It is hard to imagine that this kind of message would not be heard and acted upon by powers beyond our comprehension.

Your organization, our community and indeed the entire spiritual world are indeed fortunate to have individuals like yourself in leadership roles. The work you do is important. This event was a significant undertaking for which we are all very grateful. Let us hope that this Lighting of Hope event will actually light a beacon that continues to shine in our hearts with ongoing prayers for peace.

Carrying the Flame

Savitri

J ust over a week before the American Flame was lit, one of the big airfreight companies had provisionally agreed to carry the Flame to the UK. So confident was their representative that Lalita had relaxed her efforts to find a carrier. However, two days before the flight was due to leave on 30th June, a special board meeting of the company reversed the decision.

Lalita was devastated.

What could they do? There simply wasn't time to organise another air carrier. In this desperate situation, Mansukh suggested another solution.

Years before, he said, his father had described how the ancient traditions considered that the power of a flame rested in its wick. He went on to describe a special meditation practice that will enable you to feel as if you *are* a living flame, a living light. But it wouldn't be easy; travelling this way would require a lot of concentration for the entire journey.

Lalita was determined to do it. She had a special connection with Mansukh's father, having nursed him on his deathbed, and his memory had become a great source of strength for her. She felt sure that she could hold the meditation strongly enough to bring the Flame's essence over to the UK by herself.

So, while all the other Flames flew physically alight, the American Flame travelled within the wick of a lamp and burned within the heart of a deeply committed German woman who had grown to love America. Throughout the long hours of the journey Lalita neither slept nor ate, drinking only a small amount of water, holding the lantern close by her and keeping her awareness fixed on a light kindled within her heart.

When she finally reached the UK she had been holding her contemplation so strongly, for so long, that the moment the lamp was relit she felt herself transported back to the top of Pikes Peak. It was incredible how vivid the image was.

Later she described how the experience had changed her.

'I can't tell you how it happened, or why, but ever since that long meditation, a joy has been kindled in my heart that never goes away. Since that moment, I only have to think of the journey and I immediately feel that happiness within me. Momentary emotional ups and downs haven't really been able to touch me since. It seems strange and perhaps hard to believe but, nevertheless, it's my experience.'

For Lalita, the Flame was burning within her as a new and very real source of permanent joy.

And so the American Flame of Peace had arrived in Britain.

BRIDGING THREE NATIONS

THE CANADIAN FLAME

―

*" Our hopes are high. Our faith in the people is great.
Our courage is strong. And our dreams
for this beautiful country
will never die. "*

―

Pierre Trudeau
Former Prime Minister, Canada

Anything Is Possible

Savitri

You've got three days,' I said to Julie, knowing the impact my words would have. 'The Dutch plane leaves from Winnipeg early on Thursday morning!' It was 5th July in Eindhoven and I had just finished the meeting with the Dutch Air Force, in which they had agreed to fly a second Flame, this time from Canada. I had phoned Julie as soon as I got back to the office.

There was a long pause on the other end of the phone. Julie was thinking furiously. If we accepted the Dutch offer, it meant we had three days to transport a special safety lantern to Canada, find someone suitable to light the Flame, and then somehow get it to Winnipeg in time for Thursday morning.

Julie was not going to entertain the thought that this could not be done. The offer to fly a Flame back from Canada was an unexpected opportunity and Mansukh's father had often told us that when you are involved in an altruistic project, you should accept every offer of help that comes your way. You never know why life has sent it in your direction.

'Okay,' was all she said, but I could sense her excitement at the prospect.

Julie solves problems with a natural ease. She has learnt to step past the twin fears that normally stop people from finding the solutions they need: she isn't afraid of the solution being much larger than expected, nor does she worry about being inadequate when actually she's perfectly capable. Even when the problem seems insurmountable, she'll still put everything she's got into it. Years of humanitarian work have given her an unshakeable faith that if her goal is in harmony with the flow of life, then life itself will give her the skills and resources to get there.

Soon that was exactly what we were experiencing. After a series of opportune phone calls which seemed to lead effortlessly from one person on to the next, the team were led to Stan Williams, Chief of the Ojibwa Nation in the province of Manitoba. He had become famous for pioneering reconciliation work between First Nation peoples and other Canadians. As soon as he heard of our own work in detraumatisation and our affiliation with Gandhi, he enthusiastically offered to light the Flame.

We were struck by the perfection of it all. Less than forty-eight hours after receiving the offer from the Dutch Air Force, we not only had the lighting ceremony in place, but the man who would light the Flame was a pioneer of reconciliation work using a philosophy very similar to our own.

To witness a First Nation Elder light a sacred fire is to watch the wisdom of a thousand generations reaching out for light. Ever since the dawn of time, humans have been entranced, healed and uplifted by fire.

Stan Williams prepared for the lighting ceremony with the greatest reverence.

He began by recounting a legend from his tradition. In ancient days, he said, the Elders of his nation had described how one day seven flames would come to the earth. When these flames were joined together into an eighth flame of friendship and harmony, according to the legend, a golden age of peace would be created on earth.

He was visibly moved. He had spent years devoting his life to helping people overcome trauma and prejudice, and now he was about to light a flame that would help build reconciliation on a global scale. With great care he lit the Flame for Canada as if making a deeply-held gesture of acceptance and forgiveness, not only to those who had hurt his people, but also to the world as a whole.

With this acceptance, the Flame of Peace for Canada glowed into being, full of truth and wisdom. It had become a bridge between the First Nation and other Canadian communities.

Meanwhile, at Winnipeg, the Dutch aircraft was waiting to carry the Flame to Europe.

The plane's final destination was an airbase near Eindhoven. There, lines of soldiers wearing full combat gear were waiting to catch a flight to begin peace-keeping operations in Kosovo.

One of the soldiers in the lines saw the Flame and walked over for a closer look. 'Is that the Peace Flame?' he asked.

Apparently, news that a live Flame of Peace had arrived on a military jet had rapidly spread around the base.

'Yes—just this minute arrived from Canada,' was the reply.

The soldier's face lit up. 'I hope it works,' he said, 'because then we wouldn't need armies any more!'

At that moment, an announcement came over the loud-speakers. The flight to Kosovo had been cancelled! The soldiers in the lines picked up their guns and kit and filed away.

It felt as if the Peace Flame was already beginning its work.

The final leg of its journey to the UK was completed on Wednesday, 14th July in an aircraft that had been scheduled for a training flight that day. Lalita joined the flight and arrived in Birmingham feeling like royalty. They had flown in the Dutch Queen's private jet!

It seemed as though almost anything was possible for a person who works for a selfless cause. No amount of money can buy a ticket to travel on a royal jet, yet our friends had found all doors open, simply because of their total commitment to making the world a better place.

During the flight, Lalita looked out the window and happened to notice the silhouette of their plane on the clouds below. It was surrounded by a perfect rainbow.

The Canadian Flame had arrived in Britain.

THE SPIRIT HAS LANDED

THE JOURNEY OF THE AUSTRALIAN FLAME

" If you can dream—and not make dreams your master,
If you can think—and not make thoughts your aim,

If you can meet—Triumph and Disaster
And treat those two imposters just the same...

...Yours is the Earth and everything in it,
And—which is more—you'll be a Man, my son! "

Rudyard Kipling

Appearance of an Ancient Fire

Savitri

By the time the Canadian Flame was safely en route, the World Peace Flame project had developed into something far greater than we had ever imagined. It felt as if something new had been born, which like any growing child required a fantastic amount of attention to every minute step along the way. One moment would bring an amazing breakthrough which would have us all cheering, the next an 'impossible' new challenge to overcome. We were being stretched in every direction, forced to think in ways we'd never experienced before. But we knew we were part of something special and loved every minute of it. All we had to do was follow the remarkable opportunities we kept discovering—and keep working hard!

We now turned our full attention to the other continents. Very little progress had yet been made in Australia, and we had little more than two weeks to organise a lighting ceremony 20,000 kilometres (12,000 miles) away, as well as find a way to fly the Flame to the UK. To help her, Julie called in Cherry Knight, our Australian Co-ordinator who had just arrived back in Wales, and Trish Brown, our Volunteer Coordinator based in Canberra.

For three days they followed every lead they had, but by Monday, 12th July, there was nothing to show for their efforts.

Trish considered the options that night as she went to bed. Should she just ring Cherry and tell her it was all impossible? No. Deep inside, a firmer part within was rebelling at the idea.

At difficult times like this, Mansukh's mother would ask us, 'Are you empowering the things you are good at, or worrying about what you cannot do?' She would always say, 'Build on your strengths. What you focus on expands.'

Trish is gifted with a natural ability to trust the solid ground she has already gained and toss aside worries about the path she has yet to travel. That night as she lit a candle, she filled herself with a certainty that their efforts would succeed, and silently made a mighty plea for help.

The very next morning brought their first breakthrough. They were finally introduced to an officer in the Royal Australian Air Force (RAAF) who had the authority to help. Two days later, his office called Cherry to confirm they would fly the Flame from Sydney to the UK that coming Sunday, 18th July. The news sent cheers all around our Centre in Wales.

That left three days to organise the lighting ceremony. So far, numerous leads still hadn't produced any results. Now, however, events began to speed up and it started to feel as though we were riding on a wild river. We had reached a threshold experienced by many groups working for a cause higher than their own personal interests. The momentum generated by our efforts had suddenly become so strong we knew it would overcome all remaining obstacles.

Trish made a series of calls that Thursday morning which caught just the right person at just the right time and led her to Pearl Wymarra, an Aboriginal Elder who had just retired as Director of the Indigenous Studies Unit at the University of Western Sydney. Nationally acclaimed for her educational work, Pearl was also steeped in the traditions of her ancestors. For more than five hundred centuries they have carried fire as their most treasured possession; now she was teaching her people how to use the campfire once again for healing and rebuilding their communities. The story of the Flames struck a deep chord within her—and for more than the obvious reason.

'Just yesterday I was in despair at the constant obstacles

stopping me from helping my people,' she said. 'Last night I prayed so hard, and then accepted that after all, it is God who is in control. And now, the very next day, you are calling to invite me to light a Flame for Peace for all of Australia!' She couldn't believe the speed of the response to her predicament. 'It would be an honour to help you.'

Pearl felt it essential that the Flame lighting ceremony should bring people together. 'The Flame is the spirit of peace,' she said passionately. 'We are connected by this light, and it runs through us all. I would like all sectors of Australia's community to be involved when we light this Flame of Peace.'

She offered to call leaders of both the Aboriginal and white communities and, amazingly, all these busy people were free on the morning of Saturday, 17th July.

The ceremony had come together with ease. However, there was hardly time for celebration—the safety lantern for the Flame still hadn't arrived from America.

In order to fly a live flame on an aircraft we had to conform to the most stringent safety regulations. The lamps we had been using were the same that are used to fly the Olympic Flame. Based on the original Davey Lantern from the coal mines of Wales, they will go out rather than explode in the presence of flammable gases.

Cherry phoned the American company supplying the lanterns and discovered to her horror that a computer had malfunctioned and lost their order. The lamp had not even been sent! With no time remaining to freight another lamp, our lighting ceremony suddenly had nothing to light!

Many times during the journeys of the Flames we encoun-tered obstacles like this. We saw them as tests of our commit-ment and our skills. Thinking fast, Cherry asked the American company if they had sent any similar lamps to Australia recently. Yes, the Sydney 2000 Olympic Committee had pur-chased two lamps a few months before. A flurry of phone calls identified the man in charge of the Olympic Torch relay run around Australia, Joseph Buhagiar.

Taking a deep breath and filling herself with positivity, Cherry made the call. To her relief, Joseph was more than willing to help.

'I can't hand over our Olympic Lanterns since we need the two we have for the Run,' he said. 'However, I do know a shop in Sydney where you can buy one.'

Cherry couldn't believe it! 'All that effort,' she half laughed and half cried with relief, 'and what we needed was right there in Sydney under our noses all along.' That was the miracle of it all. Somehow everything always came together, but never a moment too soon. The suspense was often nerve-racking but fabulously exciting.

By now Cherry wasn't going to take any chances. 'Would you help us make sure the lamp works properly at the ceremony?' she asked Joseph. 'No problem,' he responded. He was planning to be in the area anyway that day.

Now everything was ready.

When Pearl Wymarra began to prepare for the ceremony, she took one look at the complex safety lantern we had bought and asked Joseph Buhagiar to take charge of it. As he began to fuel the lamp he realised it would never stay alight all the way to the UK without a crucial modification. With a wry grin to Trish and Pearl he reached into a bag and pulled out another lantern. 'I thought I'd bring a spare just in case,' he said. 'This one will last longer.' It was one of the Olympic Lanterns.

The Australian Flame would travel Olympic style after all!

The waiting crowd of media and RAAF representatives, politicians, and the public fell silent. Pearl was joined by the Mayor, leaders of the Aboriginal community—Leanne Tobin and her son, Shay, plus a young tribesman named Jackamarra—as well as Wendy Holland, the new Director of Pearl's unit at the University.

Representing young and old, indigenous and white, civic

and professional, they all thought of the ancient fires that have brought people together across the continent for millennia. They imagined all the peoples of Australasia—indigenous, white and new settlers—living together with respect, dignity and mutual support. Then, in the traditional way, they ignited a piece of bark and transferred the flame into the Lantern.

The unbounded spirit of freedom represented by the Australian Flame was now alight.

Fire is important to our people; our people
could not do without it.
Fire means:
the calling of people together,
the gathering in a circle around the fire for
cooking and eating and for warmth at night;
the gathering for ceremonies;
the gathering for story telling;
the place for being together.
Fire is at the heart of our Indigenous culture.
Aboriginal Prayer

The Six Day Journey

Savitri

B y a strange quirk of fate the Australian Flame of Peace was carried to the UK in a plane heading for the Royal Fairford Military Air Tattoo, the largest display of air force power that had ever taken place in history.

The Life Foundation team was led by Andrew and our colleague, Anita Goswami. On their arrival they were met by a public relations officer from the RAF and conducted through a maze of the most technologically advanced fighter jets in the world. Eventually, they reached the plane that had carried the Flame of Peace.

The Australian crew greeted them at the top of the stairs of their Boeing 707 after a six-day journey via the Pacific. They were filled with pride at the success of their mission. 'When we reached high altitude,' said the pilot, 'the oxygen content of the air was so low that the Flame became a very faint blue. One night I woke up in a panic and rushed over to it thinking it had gone out. But then I saw a minute cone of flame remaining.

'After that we set up a twenty-four hour watch to look after the Flame. Normally when we stop over in a country we all go out and see the sights. But this time, we couldn't bring ourselves to leave the Flame by itself. A few of us always stayed behind, just to make sure.'

When he handed the Flame over to Anita, he seemed almost reluctant to let it go. It was like watching a father wave goodbye to his child!

Carrying the Flame down the stairway, they were deafened

by a thunderous roar. 'While we had been talking with the crew,' Andrew recalls, 'the new Stealth Bomber had been making its first ever public appearance in Europe, wheeling and thundering above us. It landed on the runway next to us at *precisely* the same moment that the Flame was carried off the plane and onto British soil.'

Seconds later, the RAF public relations officer came over to the team in great excitement. He had been listening to the radio commentator through his ear-piece. 'Do you realise what has just happened?' he said. 'The American nickname for the Stealth Bomber is *The Spirit*. Just as you carried your Flame onto the tarmac, the commentator was saying on the radio, 'Ladies and Gentlemen, the Spirit has landed.'

'What an incredible co-incidence,' he said, apparently deeply moved.

The team looked at the tiny Flame of Peace burning behind its safety shields.

Yes, they thought. The Spirit had landed.

FROM
MAHATMA GANDHI

THE JOURNEY OF THE
INDIAN FLAME

"Full effort is full victory."

Gandhi

From a Poor Man's Broom

Mansukh

What could best represent a Flame of Peace for Asia? As we thought of this question, we felt that in some way or other it should involve Mahatma Gandhi. To us, his life was an ideal example of peacemaking, perfectly balancing the Eastern approach of introspection with the Western path of action. So we were delighted when my cousin, Thakor, who directs our work in India, suggested that we light the Asian Flame from the eternal flame at the M.K. Gandhi memorial in Raj Ghat, Delhi, India.

Together with a close colleague, Meetha Patel, Thakor went to Delhi to make the necessary arrangements.

Gandhi's life has always given me great hope. At the start of his career he was seen as a failure, an ineffective, anxiety-ridden young man hardly able even to argue a law case, let alone liberate a nation. Nevertheless, over a period of twenty to thirty years, he transformed himself into such a beacon of strength that he brought freedom to India and inspiration to the whole world. Day by day during this period he systematically discovered the hidden strengths we all have within. 'I have not the shadow of a doubt,' he wrote towards the end of his life, 'that any man or woman can achieve what I have, if he or she would make the same effort and cultivate the same hope and faith.'

Ever since they had known Gandhi in the 1930s and '40s, my parents had striven to live in the spirit of this great man's life of service. 'What is your message to the world?' a reporter once asked Gandhi. 'My life is my message,' was his simple yet powerful reply. Like Gandhi, my parents had learned to find their strengths within themselves, rather than depending on exterior things for their happiness. As a result they were always positive, buoyant and free, filled with amazing creativity and, most of all, endless patience.

All their lives they laboured to help others learn to do the same.

Standing before the eternal flame in Delhi, Thakor was full of his own memories of my parents and, through them, of Gandhi himself. 'What would he be doing if he were alive today?' Thakor wondered. No doubt, he would be creating programmes that would inspire millions to make a positive difference for the world.

With this in mind, Thakor approached the monument, holding our specially prepared safety lantern. Before him, flickering and dancing in a plain enclosure, was a fire that had been burning since 1948, kindled from the actual flames that engulfed the funeral pyre carrying the Mahatma's body.

As Thakor went to transfer a light from the eternal flame to his lantern he hesitated, realising the flames were too far away to reach with the short taper he was holding.

At that moment, the Government of India's Keeper of the Flame caught Thakor's eye. He walked over to a corner of the enclosure and spotted an old bamboo broom that had been left in the area. He bent down and carefully pulled a piece of straw from its bristles. Thakor received it with reverence. He thought of all the peacemakers from this ancient land—Gandhi, Ramana Maharishi, Aurobindo, Vivekananda, Sankaracarya, Buddha, Ashoka, Arjuna and Krishna and so many more—and then carefully lit the straw, lifting out a tiny flame and placing it onto the wick of the lantern.

More than sixty years before, Mahatma Gandhi had transferred his light and vision to my parents. Now his light had once again been transferred into our lives. Echoing the simplicity and service of this great man's life, the Flame of Peace for India was lit from the straw of a poor man's broom.

The radiant presence of the Indian Flame was now burning freely.

That light which resides in the sun, the moon and in fire, illuminating the whole world— know this light to be Mine.

Bhagavad Gita

A Constant Stream of Certainty

Mansukh

All the momentum being gathered by our Peace Flames project was now reaching its climax. The Flames were to be united in just over a week and a half's time and more than six hundred people were coming from all over the world to be part of the ceremony. In our busy North Wales office faxes were flying, telephones ringing frenetically and emails were pouring in. Sleeping and eating seemed unimportant; the excitement created by the arrival of each fresh piece of news was too exhilarating. We had never been so inspired.

Everything was well on the way to being completely prepared.

Except one thing. The Flame from Asia had not yet arrived, and no-one had yet agreed to fly it for us.

By this stage, defeat was inconceivable. We'd held the dream of combining the Flames so strongly and for so long that it was impossible for us to imagine any other outcome.

Nevertheless, we couldn't afford to think that we'd done enough and that a solution would somehow, magically appear. Complacency was not an option! Regardless of whether we felt we had given everything of ourselves to the project we still had to think more, feel more, and act more decisively. We tried everything we could think of.

Savitri called the very highest echelons of the Indian Air Force and found them in the midst of preparations for a possible conflict against Pakistan. They were far too busy to even think of flying a flame of peace.

Julie's team finally managed to reach a provisional agreement with Air India, subject to a go-ahead from India's air traffic controllers. But obtaining this proved difficult.

'Send me all the material,' was all the senior Controller would say. 'I'll think about it.'

The ceremony was now only eight days away and Julie's instinct told her not to wait.

'In the face of challenges like these we learnt not to take things personally,' Julie said later. 'In fact, getting emotional was always disastrous. We noticed that all the little 'coincidences' that made our project so exciting—like calling the right office at just the right time to speak to just the right person— would stop flowing the moment we got annoyed, or lost our sense of humour and lightness. So we learnt to take a step back instead and reflect creatively on what we might do next. Inevitably, a new perspective would precipitate from a completely unimagined source when we found a place of stillness within.'

So what did she do? A step back at this point seemed to mean going back to the drawing board. Julie was so determined to fly Gandhi's Flame that even at this stage she was prepared to do just that.

However, on Sunday, 25th July she received an unexpected email from Sri Lankan Airlines, who she had approached some weeks before. Having had no response from them she'd assumed they weren't interested. Now it seemed they had been considering her request all along and had agreed to transport the Flame!

Their only possible flight was due to depart from Colombo, Sri Lanka, on the morning of Wednesday, 28th July. Julie called Thakor first thing on Monday morning with instructions to drive to the nearest airport, seven hours away in Bombay.

They were tremendously excited. Falguni Patel, a Life Foundation co-worker, would travel to the UK with the Flame, accompanied as far as Colombo by Ganga Marvin, one of our senior tutors who was in India at the time.

'As soon as the journey began,' said Ganga afterwards, 'we felt enveloped in an amazing feeling of strength. It all felt so right. We *knew* that the light would travel to Britain, because we knew that Asia *had* to be represented within the World Peace Flame.'

However, when they arrived in Colombo, Falguni was refused entry. It transpired that she hadn't been granted the right visa.

'We weren't worried in the slightest,' said Ganga. 'By this time we were absolutely certain that the Flame was going to complete the journey. We just stood to one side and waited to see what would happen next. It was like watching a play unfold.'

Sure enough, a few minutes later an Englishman wearing an airline uniform walked over and introduced himself. 'Hi, I'm Ian,' he said warmly. 'I'm in charge of Aircraft Maintenance with Sri Lankan Airlines and I've been working with Julie on transporting the Flame. I'll make sure everything works out for you.'

After talking briefly with the people at Immigration, who then allowed them through, he proceeded to usher Ganga and Falguni into what looked like an engineering part of the air-port. There he showed them a special flame-safe carrying box he had just 'knocked up for the journey'. The Dutch Air Force had despatched to India one of the special boxes they had been using to transport the lamps, but it had been caught in customs and no amount of effort had been able to get it released in time. Instead, using a drawing faxed from The Netherlands to Colombo via the UK, Ian had gone far beyond the call of duty and built a replacement overnight to be ready for their flight.

On the morning of Wednesday, 28th July, Ian himself con-ducted Falguni through Departures and onto her plane. Again, there was a halt in the proceedings. No-one, it seemed, had told the pilot that a live flame would be travelling on his aircraft! Ian spent a patient fifteen minutes convincing him the mission was safe. They finally received the all-clear and the Flame of Asia was on its way.

Nothing other than pure commitment had made the journey of this Flame possible. 'There comes a time when an individual becomes irresistible and his or her action becomes all-pervasive in its effect,' wrote Gandhi. 'This comes when he reduces himself to zero.' Everyone involved in the journey of the Indian Flame had given every ounce of their strength and certainty to a cause that was much greater than themselves. As far as they could, they had removed their own agendas, doubts and fears from their work. They had never once wavered from their certainty that the Indian Flame would arrive. And so their efforts proved irresistible.

It is not often that a live flame makes its way through Security at London's Heathrow Airport. Nevertheless, late in the afternoon of Wednesday, 28th July, Falguni carried it past all the immigration checks, through customs and into the arrival hall. From there it was taken to London's largest Indian temple where it was given a royal welcome by a crowd of over one thousand people. They had gathered to celebrate the day that in the Indian tradition honours the spiritual teacher. In Sanskrit, the word for a spiritual guide is 'guru', which literally means 'remover of darkness'.

What more appropriate day could there have been for the arrival of the Indian Flame?

THE SEVENTH LIGHT

THE JOURNEY OF THE
MIDDLE EASTERN FLAME

" *The light streams toward you*
From all things, all people

From all possible permutations
Of good, evil, thought, passion

The lamps are different
But the Light is the same

The lamps are different
But the Light is the same "

Jelauddin Rumi
13th Century

With Only Hours to Spare

Savitri

H as your intuition ever told you that something should
be happening, without giving you any idea how?

In the final few weeks before the Flames were due to
be joined together I had a growing feeling that we should be
including the Middle East in our plans. However, we had
absolutely no contacts in the region and I was hesitant to start
inquiries there so late in the project in case we just ended up
with a huge waste of effort.

Not long before he died Chhaganbhai had said to me,
'When you feel that your heart is reaching out for something
new, sit in silence with your light and ask the stream of life to
guide you. Circumstances will always give you the right indi-
cations.' As a result, I took time aside to ask this silent question
on several occasions amidst all our busy preparations.

When we heard that Air India was unable to fly the Flame
from India, we had to consider the real possibility that we
should be looking elsewhere for the Asian Flame. Should a
Flame be lit in the Middle East instead of India?

I rang Colonel Harts and asked him which air force had the
largest presence in the Middle East. It was the British Royal Air
Force (RAF).

My heart missed a beat. They had not responded positively
to our initial enquiries about the Flames. Still, it was worth
another try.

'I don't suppose you know anyone there?' I asked him. To
my relief, it turned out that he happened to have a close friend

in the RAF; a senior officer based in London.

Suddenly another of those clear and open pathways began to materialise in front of us. I contacted the senior officer, who readily gave provisional authorisation. He referred me to a Squadron Leader at the RAF Lyneham airbase, who in turn asked me to fax him all the details.

On the following Monday, 26th July, I answered one of the many incoming calls we received in our office that morning. It was RAF Lyneham, giving final confirmation that they would fly a Flame from the Middle East.

It was great news but now it put us in a dilemma. Only the day before, Sri Lankan Airlines had agreed to fly a Flame from India, so we no longer needed a different Flame to represent Asia. Should we accept the RAF offer anyway? Did we need another Flame from the East at this late stage?

My intuition took over and the words flew out of my mouth before I could even think. '*Yes!* We'd like to fly that Flame!'

Within a few hours we had organised for a safety lantern to be sent out to the large British base in Bahrain, ready to be lit and then returned on a flight scheduled for later in the week.

However, late that afternoon I received a disturbing phone call. The senior safety officer at RAF Lyneham had just heard of our plans and put her foot down. Nobody was going to land a live flame at her airbase. Nothing I could say would convince her that our project was safe, regardless of how many other people had authorised it.

We phoned everyone who might be able to reassure her. However, Colonel Harts and his friend in London weren't available as each had gone away on holiday and none of the other people I had talked to had sufficient rank. The flight to Bahrain that was supposed to carry our lantern was due to leave very early on Thursday morning so we had to get clearance before the close of working hours on Wednesday.

Half way through Wednesday afternoon I rang the officer in charge of the flight.

'Personally, I see no problem,' he said, 'but what she says goes.'

'Don't leave without it,' I persisted, not willing to give up. 'It has to happen.'

'Good luck,' he said. 'You've got about two and a half hours.'

I went outside and looked up at the sky, my mind blank. We'd tried everything and found every single option closed. At the same time something inside me *knew* that the Flame was going to arrive, that it would happen. But how? Mansukh was outside with the final session of a youth retreat and they were sending a big balloon up in the air as part of their concluding celebrations. They called me over to join them but all I could think was, 'No, I want a plane in the air, not a balloon!'

Just then, someone called over from the office. 'Savitri, call for you. It's RAF Lyneham on the line.'

I raced in and picked up the phone. A voice on the other end said, 'Ms MacCuish?' The officer refusing authorisation had suddenly been called away from the base. 'If you are ready, the Flame can go ahead.'

How was it possible that circumstances could change so abruptly? What force was at work that could open people's minds to new ideas so dramatically?

That afternoon filled me with questions about the way the Flames of Peace project had so clearly gathered a life of its own.

The Sands of Bahrain

Savitri

By now it was late on Wednesday afternoon. I sat in our office with a telephone in my hand and a certainty in my heart. As far as I was concerned, the Middle Eastern Flame was now as good as home. Every fibre of my being knew it would arrive in time.

Nevertheless, the flight back from Bahrain was due to take off in just over twenty-four hours. How would we find someone there who would light the Flame?

Thousands of miles away from us, that 'someone' was out there. A few days earlier the Emir had expressed openness to the idea, but now it was much too late to get the necessary security clearances.

Eventually, as I sat in deep contemplation, I had a flash of inspiration. I picked up the phone and called the leader of the airbase in Bahrain.

'Would you be willing to light the Flame for us?' I asked.

There was a stunned silence at the other end of the phone. Finally he cleared his throat and said simply, 'I would be honoured.'

I went through the lighting procedure with him.

'First, please use a match and not a cigarette lighter.'

'Use match and not lighter,' he repeated, writing it down.

'Take the lamp outside and place it on the natural earth, not tarmac.'

'Outside… on the earth… not tarmac…' he continued, writing everything down and repeating it back to me in a matter-of-fact way.

'And can you ask everyone who is with you to pause for a moment or two and sit in silence?'

'What then?'

'Then go back and relive the moment when you first made the decision to join the Air Force. The moment you decided to offer your life so your country could stay free.'

This time there was a long silence on the other end of the phone and I could sense that this request had moved him deeply.

'As you strike the match,' I continued, 'please say, 'May all beings be at peace, and may all beings find the true peace that lies in their own hearts.' Think of all the people in the Middle East coming together in harmony. Please know that as you light this Flame you are representing all the people in those countries.'

'I will do my best,' came a very still voice from a long way away.

I put the phone down and imagined all the cultured elegance of the Middle Eastern Flame of Peace burning brightly on the sands of Bahrain.

On the afternoon of Friday, 30th July, the Middle Eastern Flame was picked up from RAF Lyneham by Derek Robertson, a former Lieutenant Colonel involved in peacekeeping operations in the Middle East. Departing early on Saturday morning he brought the Flame up to us in North Wales just hours before the ceremony to unite the Flames was due to start.

Inside the safety box that carried the Flame we found a new box of matches, with one used match inside. The label on the matchbox showed a man running with a lighted torch in his hand. On the top it said 'Marathon Major—The Best in the Long Run'. At about the same time we received a fax from Bahrain wishing us well for the Conference. The end of the fax read simply: 'Everything done as you requested... Mission accomplished.'

For me, the Middle Eastern Flame came into our lives with a will of its own that was unstoppable.

God said, 'Let there be light,'
and there was light;
and God saw that the light was good...

Genesis

JOINING THE FLAMES

THE BIRTH OF THE
WORLD PEACE FLAME

*" There is nothing more powerful
in this world than an idea
whose time has come. "*

Victor Hugo

30ᵗʰ July, 1999

Savitri

It was the night before the Flames were due to be united. In the tranquil warmth of the early evening, Mansukh and I went to visit the Flames as they rested in the main Silent Room of our Centre in the Nant Ffrancon Valley, North Wales.

The lights were turned down low, and the Flames cast a soft yellow glow around the room. There was an incredible stillness about them. Each had engineered a journey of epic proportions to arrive here, together travelling more than 65,000 km (41,000 miles) from the distant corners of the Earth. They were far more than flames burning inside safety lamps. Each of them had been lit in unique circumstances by a person filled with a desire to inspire humanity. Within its light each of the Flames carried the highest intentions of peace for a major region of the world.

Memories of Mansukh's parents filled my mind. His father had once said, 'Constantly turn your vision upwards. Should we condemn war or focus *entirely* on creating circumstances that magnify peace?' The Flames burning before us had come to inspire peace, not just between nations, but within every human heart.

Tomorrow, the Flames would be ignited together into one single World Peace Flame. The thought brought a quiver of anticipation. There was no doubt in my mind that this simple, unique act would have immense, most probably global consequences. These Flames would combine to form a living beacon for all humanity, a perpetual reminder of our innate human greatness.

We looked at each other in silent awe. What could we say that could express the magnitude of what we had before us? Many questions flowed through our hearts and minds. *Why us? Why now? Why here?* But even though we didn't have exact answers to all these questions, we were sure about one thing. All our words, all our feelings and all our actions in the last three and a half months had given rise to an authentic expression of peace. We knew it would now go on to grow and expand, helping all life on this planet to evolve towards ever greater harmony.

It was time to go. There were a myriad last-minute details to sort out before the morning. This was an event which, to our knowledge, had never happened before in the history of the world. We were eager to ensure that it would completely uplift the hearts and minds of everyone present.

My gaze lingered over the lamps one last time. I wanted to anchor their image into my mind forever.

The moment was never to repeat itself, and I heard the words of my father, saying, 'No-one stands in the same river twice.'

Mansukh

The Joining of the Flames

Mansukh

Early in the morning we moved the Flames to the site of our International Life Conference in Bangor, at the University College of North Wales.

It is an ancient site. Before the Romans came, there had been a town here. Before any of today's cathedrals had been built in mainland Britain one had been erected here. Now a great light of peace would be kindled here. We would be cradled between the sea and the mountains, our Conference site flanking the old route into the ancient Celtic landscape of Ynys Môn (Anglesey), the isle of the druids. Today, Flames from across the world would be united at one of Britain's most ancient crossroads.

Savitri, Lalita, Andrew, Anita and I, together with a group of our core team, began to prepare the Flames for the ceremony. We were filled with peace and a profound awe. When you seize and then accomplish a supremely challenging goal, your heart and mind are lifted, carried on wings beyond their own to a place of joy and calm certainty that reaches much further than words. We had done it! Filled with all the achievements of the past few months we felt completely immersed and completely in tune with the tide of life, all its challenges, all its glory, all its reality. This was the state of creativity and peace we hoped would one day be set free by the Flame we were about to bring into life.

We picked up the tall, shiny Olympic-style torches which would carry the Flames and carefully began to transfer the light from each lamp onto them. As we ignited each torch, a burst of light seemed to travel far beyond the limits of the room, filling our thoughts with each great region of our planet in turn: Africa. Australasia. Europe. India and the Middle East. Canada and the USA.

Annie Jones, the Conference Master of Ceremonies, had prepared the scene well, and as we entered the Conference Hall, six hundred people rose as one. People from around the world—doctors, tradesmen, mothers, politicians, therapists, religious leaders, young people, artists and so many others—would be witnessing this once-in-a-lifetime moment.

Flanked by flags from the continents of the Flames we were carrying, we walked slowly into the Conference Hall. The journey from the back of the room to the stage was like ascending an invisible ladder of awareness. It seemed to take a lifetime, our perceptions and inner senses heightening with every step. It was timeless, effortless, yet fully charged with the simple act of planting one foot in front of another. An immense feeling of belonging enveloped us all.

Many things passed through my mind in those incredible moments. We were excited, elated at what we had achieved, yet full of stillness. I remember thinking that truly it is the journey in life that is important, and not just the destination. Here, right here in every step, is where the Mystery sits, waiting for us to touch it. It lies in the very midst of life, not in running away from its challenges but in reaching out positively into every magnificent moment. As we held our torches, so focused, so calm, yet so excited, all the corners of life converged into a single heart beat. For a few moments—perhaps half an hour—we were one person, one breath, one flame.

I followed Savitri, Lalita, Andrew and Anita onto the stage.

My mentors used to say, 'There are no errors in the system, we are all conduits of perfection.' This was one of those times when perfection was blatantly obvious to us. The scene, the atmosphere and the event all seemed to be perfectly set. It left us all breathless.

We approached the great bowl which was awaiting the Flames and prepared to touch our torches to it in unison. All our friends in the audience focused their love and their yearning for peace onto the glowing flames we held in front of us. Everyone held their breath. Slowly, we brought the Flames down, down, towards… contact!

A plume of fire rose brightly up through the centre of the ring of flames we had created, sending a shockwave of light out across the Hall. The whole room fell into a deep silence, the only movement coming from the flickering warmth of the new creation shimmering before us.

We gazed into this new light, trying to sense, to feel and to understand what lay within its molten heart. Images of people across the continents filled our minds. We thought of all the people who had made this moment possible. Scenes of pilots, airport officers, mayors, majors, eminent peacemakers, indigenous leaders, politicians, spiritual heads and so many others flashed across our minds. What made all these people say 'yes' for no gain of earthly prestige or fame? We stared into the single Flame before us, lost in gratitude for the efforts of everyone who had helped make its journey possible.

Somewhere far beyond the reaches of thought, each of us in the room that day felt a portion of the infinite come and rest lightly upon our lives. For many it simply came and then went, like the passing of a feather in the breeze. Yet for others it landed and took root, opening up whole new vistas in their lives. A few, a very few, of these stories are related in this book.

The World Peace Flame had been born. From one moment to the next the empty bowl had become filled with a mighty column of light. My parents would have said, 'Peace is like that. Like flicking a light switch or striking a match, it takes no effort at all to fill a room with light. All you need to do is make the decision to begin.'

In just the same way, it had taken no effort at all to fill this bowl with the fire of peace. One day, we hoped, the world would find peace with exactly the same ease.

Now a new phase of the adventure would begin, as people took lights from this Flame and presented them to their friends and colleagues. From this moment, it would begin to spread out across the world, as people installed it in their hearts and minds, and cities and governments installed it in the world's centres of decision making.

Like a new sun arriving to shed its light on a world searching for answers, the World Peace Flame was ready for this new and even greater phase of its journey.

May all beings be at peace.
May all beings discover the True Peace
that lies within their own hearts.

Chhaganbhai and Ecchaben Patel

PART 2
EMPOWERING STORIES

OF HOPE, COURAGE & INSPIRATION

*" Use the light within you to regain
your natural clarity of sight.*

Seeing into darkness is clarity.

Knowing how to yield is strength.

*Use your own light and return to
the source of light.*

This is called practising eternity. "

Lao Tzu

HOW LIGHT AND THE WORLD PEACE FLAME
HAVE TRANSFORMED PEOPLE'S LIVES

- ◖ The Secret Power of Light

- ◖ Designing My Success

- ◖ Healing ~ Overcoming Tragedy

- ◖ With Children and the Family

- ◖ At Work or Study

- ◖ Building Unity and a Team that Excels

" *Let the Inner Light guide you and keep you on the narrow and straight path.* "

Mohandas K. Gandhi

THE SECRET POWER OF LIGHT

“ When we light a flame of peace,
We ignite the power and strength within us
To overcome every trial and tribulation,
The courage to turn anger into opportunity
And to turn rejection and betrayal
Into a personal awakening
Of our own inner resource of love. ”

Annie Jones,
Director, Life Foundation UK

My Parachute Jump

'Come to the edge,' he said.
'No, we are afraid.'
'Come to the edge,' he said.
They came, he pushed them... and they flew.

Guillaume Appollinaire

In this story, a series of 'fortuitous' events combine to enable this young Scottish woman to take her dream and fly with it—literally! Notice the attitudes by which she precipitated these events. While her goal may have been relatively small in the great scheme of things, the lessons she learned have the power to help each of us attain our goals. This is what she says:

'How can I make my life more special?'
When you ask yourself a question like that you have to be ready for anything.

Straight away an idea came to me; 'What if I left my car behind and walked to work at the factory?'

I'd asked myself a question, so now I had to follow my own advice! From then on I began the one-hour journey to work on foot. Soon, I discovered with delight, each day's walk turned into a kind of magical 'travelling meditation'.

On one particularly memorable day I arrived at work in the midst of an incredible symphony of bird song. My heart opened so much that I felt I could accomplish anything. Only an hour or so later, a young man named Nick approached me and asked about the Dru Yoga classes I'd just started. I told him all about them and then, with all the inspiration I'd got from my walk, I gave him a candle lit from the World Peace Flame. I could see he was really touched.

Two days later I was working on his section. As soon as he saw me he came over and explained that he and his friends were organising a parachute jump for charity. Would I like to take part as well?

'Nick,' I said, hardly able to contain myself, 'that is a dream I've had ever since I was young!' It was a complete surprise. I had always wanted to do a parachute jump and never really known how to go about it. I am a very shy person by nature, and would never have thought of making the effort to do such a thing by myself. Now, out of the blue, it seemed my dream was about to come true. I knew it was happening because of all the inspiration he and I had experienced when I gave him the World Peace Flame two days previously.

The following week I was going to North Wales for Pathfinders, a life-adventure course I attend every year. I spoke about it there, and someone said, 'Why don't you ask a company to sponsor your parachute jump?' So, once I got back to work after my course I went straight to the Director's office and chapped[1] on his door. I had presented him with the World Peace Flame a few months before and he had been very moved by the story of its creation and the way the air forces had worked with the Life Foundation. So this time, he was immediately receptive and invited me straight in. I explained all about the factory boys organising the jump and how it had always been a dream of mine. I knew he could feel that my words were coming straight from my heart. He said, 'Sarah, do you think it's fate?' and I said, 'Yes.'

With that, he agreed to sponsor me!

Whenever I work with the World Peace Flame, things just

---

[1] 'Chapped' is a Scottish word meaning 'tapped'.

seem to fall into place, if only I have the courage to take the steps forward. My experience on the Pathfinders course had propelled me to the next stage of fulfilling my dream. Much later, during my training for the jump, someone told me that parachutes had different names. I asked him the name of the one I was using. It was called the 'Pathfinder'. I knew I was on the right track!

The date the factory boys had organised for their jump turned out to be unsuitable for me so I had to make all my arrangements separately.

All sorts of obstacles came up as I got closer to the jump but, whereas in the past I might have given up, I just kept going in my confidence in the World Peace Flame. I was determined to achieve my dream. I took the Flame along with me to the training days and my teacher was very impressed by it. It was more than my mascot; it was my friend and guiding light.

Once, at the end of a long training day, I was suspended from the ceiling, trying to learn a particular trick for dealing with my parachute in an emergency. Everyone was in a hurry to leave so they could go to the pub. I took ages to get it right and eventually they became so impatient that they told me to forget trying to go solo, saying I could just as easily go for the tandem jump (when you jump with your instructor) and it would save everybody time. I felt hurt by their reactions but I was determined to push through. I told them that this moment was far more important than any pub, even though I knew the man who ran the pub was there in the room! It took me great courage to speak my truth. Nevertheless, I pressed on. I made them show me the tactic again until I got it.

Everything began to flow easily then. The company allowed me to go to all the shifts so that I could ask everybody for sponsorship and in the end I raised more than £1,100 for charity.

Eventually, I went up and made my jump.

I will never forget the feeling as I launched out of that plane. I was fulfilling a long cherished dream and had successfully overcome every barrier to get there. There was no fear in me at all as I jumped, no pounding of the heart, no butterflies in the tummy. I just sailed through, with the feeling that I was being guided through everything. I was so still, so peaceful, so supported. Other parachutists seemed to want to jump for the buzz but I just felt relaxed and calm.

Why did I feel so at ease? I am certain that it was because I was doing my jump for others. I would never have had the courage to overcome all those fears if I had been doing it all just for me. Every day I light my World Peace Flame and connect with my light and my strength. It has shown me that when you do things selflessly your dreams become reality.

I made a perfect landing. The peace and tranquillity and the feeling of total support throughout was incredible. I felt as if I was surrounded by angels' wings. It was like coming to the edge. I came, he pushed me and I flew.

S.L., Scotland

How did Sarah manage to jump into thin air without the slightest bit of fear? How can any of us stay absolutely calm in the face of something so completely beyond our comfort zones?

Three elements overcome the fear that stands in the way of attaining our dreams.

- ❖ *Sarah prepared herself well by facing and overcoming all her little fears and barriers along the way. Many one percent steps prepare you for a single one hundred percent leap later on.*
- ❖ *She was convinced she was doing the right thing because she was doing the jump for others, rather than herself.*

❖   *A great sage once said, 'The more we care about the
      wants, needs and happiness of others, the more our own
      inner peace expands and fills our being.' When peace fills
      us, there is no room available for fear.*

*By the time she jumped out of that plane, every part of her was
in harmony. When there is no conflict between the parts of us that
'know', 'think', 'feel' and 'act', then all fear disappears and is
replaced instantly by a feeling of being supported by a force
greater than ourselves. At that moment, we can accomplish anything.*

The Lamplighters

Sometimes you have to travel the world to discover the truths about the country you live in. One summer, we visited Toronto, Canada, as part of a world tour.

There we came across the remarkable story of the Lamplighters Movement during World War II. This movement is perhaps one of the world's greatest examples of the power light has to help people achieve their highest potential.

In the early days of World War II when the Battle of Britain was at its height, the war was not going well for the British. The Allies were retreating and the Blitz was causing untold suffering in London, Birmingham and other major cities. People were beginning to wonder how long they could hold out, and Churchill was calling it Britain's 'darkest hour'.

In the midst of this desperate time, one of Britain's top R.A.F. officers, Air Vice-Marshall Dowding, made an appeal to the British people.

He asked everyone to light a candle or a lamp every night at the same time. He invited people to focus all their love and prayers onto the candle and to visualise their loved ones in active service being surrounded by its light and protected by its strength.

His appeal, which became known as the 'Lamplighters Movement', was taken up by millions of people over the next few years. Their candles gave warmth and courage during the long hours of the night as people lay in bed listening for air

ness. I would do a little bit of yoga and then sit and try hard to push out the pain from my mind and emotions. It felt like holding back a huge dam. One day it was sure to break! I sat for a few minutes every day, morning and night, and just stared at the flame. Then I would close my eyes and see it flickering inside—behind my eyelids. But still the pain was there and it raged long and strong!

One morning I sat as before and this time the feeling of pain became so strong that it felt as if I was going to burst. In fact, I did burst. All I can remember is an explosion of tears mixed with enormous anger and a very deep fear. I was afraid of being completely lost. I was afraid of dying. I couldn't understand it. Why was this happening? What was I to do? Where should I go?

Suddenly, in the midst of this lowest-of-the-low experience, I heard a voice. It was quiet, it was loving and it seemed to come straight from the flame. It was also a physical feeling that went directly into my heart from the flame, like a pushing and then painless piercing into the chest cavity. It said, 'Don't you understand? *I* am calling you. I can give you what you want *and* what you need.' And then it added, '*I* want you.'

I knew that I had heard this message clearly. It was not my voice, nor anyone else's that I could recognise. It was a voice of infinite harmony, and I realised I was hearing the words of my deepest self, reflected back to me through the light of the flame in front of me. It was telling me that there was a place deep within my heart where I could experience infinite strength and infinite love. I knew I need never feel lonely again.

From that moment on my life changed. I cannot simply say that my perception changed—my whole life as I knew it and my whole understanding of myself turned around 180 degrees. My fear of what was to come changed into an excitement. I found the courage to take the decisions I hadn't yet been able to face.

I began to create a new life, far more fulfilling and rewarding than I had ever known before. I took up my yoga teaching qualification and began to care for others around me rather than focusing on my own problems. The more I did this, the more I discovered that my own problems became smaller and my experience of life became larger. I was learning how to live in a completely new way. Possibilities opened before me and the rage and anger began to fade as I found the energy and confidence to explore things I had not done before. I no longer needed a relationship to sustain me because I had found an inner sustenance.

I moved from the city into the countryside—something I had always been afraid to do because of the fear of being alone. Now that feeling no longer existed. I felt upheld and support-ed by a strong force within myself.

It has taken me a long time to understand the strength I gained that day from my prayer and meditation with a flame. Now I know that it is the experience of being an invincible being—invincible against those that can attack us from outside and invincible against the voices that can attack us from with-in.

I continue to focus on a flame every morning and night and remember that voice in my most vulnerable moments. It has become an ever-available reminder that inside there is always somewhere I can feel safe, wanted, loved and upheld—and completely indestructible.

Rupali, England

Mansukh's mother used to say, 'All you have to do is to light a candle, stop and gaze at its beauty and sooner or later it will start talking to you. Then you begin to receive support, promptings and

instructions that give you confidence and overwhelming joy in the way you design your life.'

What is happening?

Light is an ancient archetype that symbolises our highest, transcendent sources of strength, wisdom and greatness. When we fill our awareness with light we open a doorway into the very strengths this archetype represents.

From this essential beginning, all manner of new possibilities arise.

Civilisation

On the path to understanding and mastering life, it is important to realise the power of our own thoughts as well as the effect of other people's thoughts upon us. Louise Rowan, the co-ordinator of the Life Foundation's work in Canada, is an expert in this. Lively and vivacious, she is also profoundly sensitive to the needs of others, and here shows us one example of how we are all connected.

In one of my favourite cities in Europe there is an eternal Peace Flame that has been burning for many years. It burns in the open, surrounded by fountains of water, and thousands of people travel past it every day on their way over one of the bridges into the downtown area.

One summer I arrived back in Europe after a long absence and could immediately feel that something had changed in the city. There was a lot of unrest, the streets felt less safe and many of the people in caring professions were highly stressed. On investigation I discovered that a new government had come to power and dramatically cut benefits for the poorer section of society, with the result that the streets in one part of the city had become the home for many hundreds of homeless people who now had nowhere to go. I was amazed. How could this possibly happen? The city has always had a reputation for being extremely liberal and caring.

Then I visited the Flame. I couldn't believe what I saw. In place of the proudly burning Flame was a derelict monument, sad and neglected, surrounded by litter. The Flame had not burnt for months, and an incredible feeling of desolation filled the scene.

I have read that many great civilisations throughout history have had eternal flames, but as soon as their flame was extinguished it was only a matter of time before their empire began to crumble. I found it interesting that the Flame had gone out a few weeks before the elections that brought this new government to power.

Five months later, on my return to Europe after a round of teaching engagements in California, I received an excited phone call from one of my students there. She was a single mother and had been particularly affected by the government's cuts. I had counselled her many times through the extreme difficulties she faced. Now she was crying in excitement so much that I could hardly make out her words. Eventually she managed to say that the unbelievable had happened. By some miracle the government had decided to modify its changes and reintroduce some of the benefits it had scrapped.

For some reason that I still can't explain, the first thing that jumped into my heart and mind was the Flame. I put down the phone, drove across the bridge and there before my very eyes, burning in its *full glory*, was the Flame of Peace.

I screeched to a halt in the car and cried with gratitude for the perfection and unity of it all. The area all around the monument was now well tended and well used, and a warm, inviting atmosphere filled the surroundings. I was thrilled at the synchronicity of the experience.

My mind went back two months to the time when Mansukh and Savitri had been in Europe with the World Peace Flame. They had brought the Flame to this very spot as part of one of their walks to bring light and healing into the world.

We are never really alone, except when we close our hearts and choose to miss the splendour of life all around us. We are linked to each other in ways that defy explanation and transcend thought. I believe that when the aspirations of each indi-

vidual in a city resonate with care and respect for all, a miniature 'Flame of Peace' is kindled not just in a monument by a
bridge, but also in the hearts of every person in the region.
Such a city, I feel sure, would last forever.

Louise Rowan, Canada

*We are all connected. At any moment the state of my mind and
yours can be resonating with, and affecting, the minds of the people around us.*

*Knowing this principle helps you make successful relationships
at work or at home. If you want positivity, agreement, respect and
concern from someone, then try to fill your mind with these qualities whenever you think about them. As a result, you will surely
inspire the very same qualities within them.*

Why Not Me?

In 1996 we were returning from Bosnia on our 'Eurowalk' tour, after running a series of seminars in that war-torn land to help people heal their emotional trauma.

As a symbol of peace and healing, we had decided to give out candles to everyone we met on the way home, asking them to light the candles all at the same time and pray for peace.

Ron, age 67, joined us near the end of this journey in a seminar organised especially for men. As you read his story, try to sense something even greater than the amazing transformation he experienced. What made it possible in the first place?

J ust before lunch, I was sitting in the audience listening to the speaker. Initially I was less than three yards from him and could clearly see his face. I could understand him well. But then he moved and stood in front of the window, and all I could see was his silhouette. I could no longer comprehend a thing.

You see, lip-reading is my communication lifeline. I have been profoundly deaf for fifty-four years, since I was thirteen. Even hearing aids can't help me.

Sitting in sudden isolation, I began to feel dejected and despondent. I had been looking forward to hearing new ideas on how men could develop their own unique strengths, and was eager to explore this in my own life. Now, however, I felt as if I had lost all chance of gaining anything from the seminar.

I began to slide down the slippery slope that beckons so

invitingly to many deaf people. I felt more and more worthless and irrelevant by the minute, lost and alone in a world that runs on sounds. Before long, I found myself wondering what the hell I was doing there and questioning why I had bothered to come in the first place.

I picked up a piece of paper that had been lying on the floor and began to idly turn it around in my hands. In my depressed state there wasn't much else to do.

After some time I began looking at the paper more carefully. Printed on one side was a picture of a candle and the words, 'Please light me for peace in Bosnia at 9.30 a.m. on Sunday, 4th August.' Then it added, 'You do make a difference.'

I read it again in stunned disbelief. I was born on 4th August, at precisely 9.30 a.m.

The paper was a wrapping for candles the seminar team were giving out along their route from Bosnia to the UK. They were asking people to light candles at the same time to create a river of light stretching all the way across Europe.

I was thunderstruck. Here in my despondency a piece of paper had come to me saying, 'You do make a difference,' with my very own birth time printed on it. I knew it was a very personal message, yet at first I could hardly grasp its magnitude. All I could be sure of was that this was no coincidence. The chances against it happening were just too great.

I asked Mansukh, one of the speakers at the seminar, why on earth this message had been so particularly addressed to me. 'Why *me*?' I questioned.

'Why not?' he responded.

It really made me think. Why not me?

Perhaps because of my lifetime of deafness, I had become very diffident about my own abilities. A deaf person like me only receives about a third of people's communications accurately, and has to intuit the rest. It is so easy to butt in at the wrong moment and make the most embarrassing mistakes. You soon learn to lie pretty low.

Now, here was life itself, some vast force that I could perhaps call God, saying, 'Yes, this is you. You are important. You are worthy of attention.'

In that moment, I became aware of my own worth for the very first time.

A gathering joy began to well up within me as these new realisations swept through my mind. I felt the weight of years of unworthiness falling away. For the first time in my life I heard my own voice within saying to myself, 'You *are* worthy!'

I was exultant and inexpressibly happy. I had discovered a world of rich new possibilities and I was eager to explore it. My despondency was gone; I had indeed gained what I came for, and much, much more.

I got onto the train home after the seminar that day feeling on top of the world. I had discovered a new and more ultimate source of peace than I had ever realised existed. I was so exuberant that I felt like standing up on the train and shouting out to everyone in the carriage, 'Hey, life is for *living!*'

More than seven years later, I still keep my piece of paper. It has become a sort of talisman, a reminder of one of the greatest turning points of my life. Whenever I feel down, which happens increasingly rarely now, I take it out and think, 'Well, this is me. I am important!'

I didn't quite overcome my English reserve enough to shout out my joy to the whole carriage on that train ride home, but I did notice people looking at me with interest throughout the journey. For the first time in my adult life, I felt I was somebody special.

And just thinking this way made it so.

Ron, England

Here is a far-reaching discovery. If life itself was able to remind Ron of his own worth—just when he most needed to hear this—is it possible the same could happen for you?

Perhaps, if ever you are feeling unsure about yourself, all you need to do is make space and listen.

Sit by a flame for a few moments every day and repeat an affirmation like Ron's. For example, you might choose to affirm, 'I do make a difference.' Write it on a piece of paper and pull it out whenever you feel down or unworthy of a task. Remember Ron's experience. If the forces of life consider him to be worthy, they certainly feel the same about you.

Encounter with a Miner

Sometimes, when we are walking towards our goals, inexplicable events bring us up short and remind us that we live in a larger and more wonderful universe than the one in which we conduct our day-to-day 'busy-ness'.

Mansukh's father used to say that every moment brings us clues telling us which direction to take next in order to create the most healing and lasting joy in our lives. Often, as this story suggests, we can find these clues by simply pausing long enough to take delight in the unexpected.

Very soon after the World Peace Flame was created, I went home to north-east England, taking with me a miniature miner's lamp lit from the Peace Flame itself. One day, my friend Joan and I went for a walk around my home city of Newcastle, carrying my lamp. This unusual sight attracted so many people who stopped and talked with us that our walk took far longer than anticipated. As we neared the end of the day we decided to catch the metro home.

This decision turned an enjoyable day into a magical one.

We sat down gratefully in the train and put the Flame down on a seat next to us. After a few minutes the train went into a tunnel and the driver failed to turn on the lights—the whole carriage was plunged into darkness, scaring some of the children. In the blackness the only light remaining was my tiny World Peace Flame lantern. In delight I picked it up and held it high in the aisle. Soon everyone was looking at the little pinpoint of light I held, and exclaiming to each other.

A moment later we were back in daylight and so I put the Flame to the side again. Joan and I thought to ourselves, 'Oh, that was rather special.'

Not long afterwards we entered another tunnel. Again the lights stayed off and again the only light relieving the darkness was the Flame as I held it up. I sensed how its presence created a wave of relief through the carriage and there were murmurs of 'Oh, yes!!' The children were this time delighted by the light and its flickering play.

We went through several more tunnels and each time the same thing happened. We found ourselves wondering about the uncanny coincidence of 'just happening' to bring a lantern onto a train that had malfunctioning lights.

Finally, we arrived in Newcastle Central underground station. The station itself was lit, but there were still no lights on the train except our Flame. We stood up in the semi-darkness to great applause from the other passengers and began to walk off. At the precise moment that we carried the Flame off the train, *all the lights on the train came on again!*

We looked at each other, stunned. 'We couldn't have organised that if we'd tried,' we said a little shakily to each other.

But this amazing day with the Flame was not yet finished. As we stood on the platform, wondering what the meaning of our strange experience might be, an old man spotted our lamp and came over. He was an ex-miner, probably in his seventies, his face lined by years of hard and dangerous work. He was very curious about our lamp.

We talked for a few moments, and then it occurred to me to ask about his experiences with light in the darkness of a coal mine.

'Could you see what you were doing, down there in the dark?' I asked. 'Did your lamp provide enough light for you to work by?'

I was not prepared for the simple depth of his answer. He

stood very still for a few moments and then said quietly, 'When you're in total darkness even the smallest light makes a difference.'

We paused, humbled. This old man had given us wisdom borne out of his experience of working in the dark for year after year in order to provide coal for fuel and light for other people. I thought of the anxiety and fear he must so often have experienced down there in the dark. One little flicker of light was enough to bring him hope.

And suddenly, I knew the secret of why the lights had behaved so strangely on the train.

Brendha, Wales

We once asked Mansukh's father to tell us the meaning of the messages that often come to us hidden in everyday events. 'Ah,' he twinkled. 'At least you are seeing them. Good.'

And that was all he would say. It was infuriating—until we realised that he was insisting that we work these things out for ourselves.

Deep and profound silence, practised regularly, is the best tool we have found for developing the sensitivity necessary to interpret the deeper meaning behind everything that happens to us.

Sixty Days to the End of the War

We have seen how light can open a new doorway to our own immense potential. How then can we use this knowledge to create effective and far-reaching success? As you'll read in this remark-able experience from our work in the mid 1990s, some of these methods are so powerful their influence may extend far beyond the boundaries of our own individual lives.

B y the summer of 1995, the Bosnian war had been dragging on in the east of Europe for nearly four years. The never ending news reports of atrocities and suffering were beginning to drive us all to distraction. Here was a war happening right on our doorstep, only a day's drive away. It was brutal and unjust beyond words and yet we felt powerless to do anything about it. Something had to change!

At the Life Foundation, we had organised food collections for Bosnia at supermarkets, canvassed hospitals for medical supplies, and now we were planning to send a group there in the following year to lead some of our detraumatisation work-shops. Yet we knew there must be more we could do.

The catalyst for change came in July 1995. We'd just finished our International Conference and welcomed a team of walkers back from Auschwitz, where they had spent ten days in work-shops and peace vigils to mark the ending of World War II in 1945. On the way home the walkers had given out candles to passers-by, asking them to light them at the precise moment they were to walk into the Conference. The result was a river of light, created on 29th July, 1995, all the way across Europe. It was a striking image of peace that caught the imagination of everyone involved.

Somehow it felt natural to turn this experience towards Bosnia.

Only a few months earlier, we had come across the idea of holding a candle flame vigil around the clock as a way of focusing our thoughts and intentions on peace. We decided to experiment. At the very least, we felt, it would give us all the opportunity to make a difference for those beleaguered people, even if we would never know the actual effect of our efforts.

It was all very new. We weren't even sure that we could sustain a continuous twenty-four hour peace vigil for very long. As we discussed various possibilities, John Jones, the Life Foundation's senior meditation trainer, suggested we begin for a fixed length of time, and then review it after that. We decided to start with sixty days.

So we picked a date to start the vigil, and all got together for a momentous evening of songs, prayers and meditations for peace on Sunday, 6th August, 1995. From then on, we created a rota so that at least one person would be sitting by the flame twenty-four hours a day.

The next weeks involved some of the most profoundly moving experiences many of us had ever had. Sitting there—often in the middle of the night—alone and at prayer in front of that little candle, we would feel ourselves gathered up into a great wind of strength and light. It would hold us in silent passion for peace, seemingly all by itself, as we poured out our hearts to people half a continent away.

As the days turned to weeks, our twenty-four hour vigil became a 'normal' part of life. We would take our turns on the rota, emerge uplifted by the experience, and then get on with our busy lives.

And in the world outside, peace negotiations came and

went. The siege of Sarajevo seemed to get worse and worse.

Then, in September, NATO sent in its jets, and the siege of Sarajevo began to collapse. Negotiations intensified and hopes for a ceasefire swung back and forth like a wild pendulum. Delegates flew to Dayton, Ohio, for talks and gradually hopes for peace began to rise.

For most of the time we didn't pay too much attention to these political developments. There had been so many failed negotiations over the years that it seemed better to concentrate on our own activities rather than pin our hopes on events so far away. We would just go to our candle, send our thoughts of peace to the people of Bosnia, and then go back to work, or to sleep, or to whatever else we were doing at the time.

And then a real ceasefire came.

I will never forget the day. It was a bright sunny morning somewhere near the beginning of October 1995. I was reading a newspaper in the car, en route from town to our retreat centre in the mountains. The paper was full of it. The Dayton negotiations had worked. A ceasefire had been agreed!

I read the text avidly. The ceasefire was provisional, it seemed, and was to be re-evaluated after sixty days.

'Sixty days?' I thought. 'That sounds familiar. Didn't we set up our peace vigil for sixty days?' The vigil seemed so much part of life now that its origins back in the summer had begun to get a little bit hazy. 'I wonder...' I thought. 'Today is 5th October. What if...?'

I did the calculations. It was precisely the sixtieth day since our vigil had begun.

The news filled us with awe. Our vigil for sixty days had ended on the very day that peace was declared for sixty days. And, as it turned out, this time the ceasefire stayed intact. The war had ended.

We will never know what part our efforts played in helping to conclude this terrible war. Life is not like that—it does not produce big neon signs emblazoned across the sky to tell you whether or not your prayers have been successful. Yet all of us who shared the experience of sitting by that little flame, wrapped up in wave after wave of strength and focus, look back on the experience with a certainty in our hearts.

We did make a difference.

Andrew Wells

Goethe said, 'Were the eye not of the sun, how could we behold light? If God's might and ours were not as one, how could his work enchant our sight?'

Within the rhythm of his words lies the most important insight we need when we want to achieve a goal: each of us carries within us an unbounded potential for co-creating our world.

Light helps you access your infinite potential. A desire to add to the greater whole enables this potential to flow out from you. Then you will find, as we did, that doorways open that are far wider than you could possibly imagine.

DESIGNING MY SUCCESS

" *I welcome this wonderful initiative of the World Peace Flame. Peace can never be taken for granted.*

It requires a stronger spirit than war to build and sustain universal co-operation, respect for life and for difference, social justice and the sharing of wealth.

Most of all, becoming a light for peace demands that each and every one be committed to a better world. We must all passionately work to become peacemakers within ourselves and in the lives of others. "

Member of Canadian Parliament

From the Factory Floor

Great opportunities are often only a question away. Here three
powerful questions and some creative proactive steps enabled
Sarah to achieve something she would never have dreamed she
could have reached a few years before.

I am normally very, very shy. I would never dream of asking
my supervisor at work for something special, never mind
going straight to the top. But last year at the big biscuit factory
where I work I found myself in it up to my neck.

One evening I heard that some friends of mine were helping
to host an interfaith gathering for 15,000 people with the World
Peace Flame. They wanted everyone to have a peace candle
and a little packet of food. So far they had got candles donated
but hadn't succeeded with the food. The words, 'Oh, I work in
a biscuit factory. I can do that,' were out of my mouth before I
had time to think.

Suddenly, timid little me had just landed herself with getting the biscuits—15,000 of them. What on earth was I going to
do?

Mind you, I was beginning to change. I'd started teaching
yoga and my classes were going really well. I had been passing
around World Peace Flame candles to all sorts of people for a
couple of years and had been lighting my own candle every
day. I could feel the strength of its light growing inside me and
felt I was ready to be a new kind of woman.

Well, next morning I went into my factory, walked straight

up to my supervisor and said, 'I need 15,000 biscuits by next Wednesday.' You should have seen her face! She told me it would be impossible.

For someone like me this should have been the end. But this time was different. I felt inspired and empowered to stand up for what I believed in. So, I said that if she could not help I would go straight to the top and speak to the Director. I was so enthusiastic about the idea of all the religions coming together that I felt sure he would agree—who wouldn't?

I started my work, still bubbling with excitement about the idea. Douglas, one of the electricians, stopped for a chat. He said he was going to be helping with a special promotion in which our company was putting a sample of one of our new biscuits through the letter boxes of a million people. That was the opening I needed. I thought, 'If my company can afford this, then it can certainly spare 15,000 biscuits for my event!'

As soon as I could get a break I told Dick Evans, our factory manager, all about it. I said I would go right to the top to get this through. I told him all about the event and the World Peace Flame and how important it would be for our company to be a part of something that was bringing so many people together in peace. I felt a grace flowing through me and could see the power of my words bringing about a complete transformation. I heard myself say, 'I'm a girl who believes in going straight to the top when you want things done fast.'

Before I had a chance to regret these challenging words, he went straight to the Director and spoke on my behalf.

I don't know how I got through the rest of that day. But the moment when my supervisor came to me the next day will stay with me for the rest of my life. She told me that the Director had told her to take over my job for a while so that I could go to the warehouse and select the biscuits I needed! Only yesterday she had told me it would be impossible! I almost danced towards the warehouse, feeling that something magical was happening. I could see things so clearly. I felt as though I was part of a miraculous play—I was in it but not of it. It was an amazing feeling.

I arrived in the warehouse wondering whether things could get any better. They could! Reg, who worked in the stores area, showed me two pallets with more than 22,000 biscuits on them. The Director had phoned to say that I could have—the lot!

There is no doubt in my mind that the power of prayer and lighting my Peace Flame every day made the impossible possible. I had gained so much peace and certainty that I knew I now had the courage to follow my heart and speak my truth come what may. I was no longer afraid of other people's appearances or status. Yippee!

Sarah, Scotland

Laurel Lee said: 'I know I am not seeing things as they are. I am seeing things as I am!' Sarah had learned to see the world from a point of courage and faith in herself.

Three factors contributed to her success.

- ❖ *She was very clear about her goal, and wasn't going to give up on it—not for anything, and most especially not for her own fears.*
- ❖ *She learnt that people are people no matter what their role. Everyone responds to sincerity, enthusiasm and a bold and infectious dream. There was no doubt that Sarah had all three!*
- ❖ *She had faith in her own strength. Once her practices with the World Peace Flame had given her enough evidence that she could stand on her own strengths, there really was no stopping her.*

The Switch

If you want to be in charge of your own destiny, remember the important choice highlighted in this charming illustration.

My friend Sheila is sixty years old. Of course, she hasn't always been sixty, just as her three grown-up sons haven't always been big! They were once her little boys and she was once their young mother. Nowadays, they wouldn't dream of asking her to tell them a story or tuck them up in bed, but it wasn't always so. There was a time when they wouldn't contemplate going to bed without one of their mother's stories and then some of her kisses…

That was a long time ago, of course… when Sheila's 'big' boys were scared of the dark! And at that time, when their Mummy's night time story finished and her kisses were still warm on their smooth cheeks the boys would shout to Sheila as she walked towards the bedroom door, hand ready to trip the light switch… *'No Mummy!* Don't switch the dark on when you go!!'

L.v.K., The Netherlands

Whatever you do, don't switch on the dark!

How often have you been completely happy, ready for anything... and then one little negative thought crept in and before you knew it you were plunged into the morass?

A constant practice of connecting to the highest part of you—or your 'light within'—is the answer given by all the great spiritual traditions to helping you keep your lights on!

At the Pentagon

One of the great keys to effective relationships—and therefore your own success and happiness—lies in learning how to help every person you meet move a little further along their own path. Watch how this happened for Ned.

One September I received an invitation to bring the World Peace Flame into the Pentagon. I must admit I was pretty sceptical at first. How could anything peaceful occur within this centre of world military might? Consequently, full of pre-judgements, I set off with my Flame on the half hour journey from where I was living in Virginia.

I had been invited to be part of a peace and interfaith ceremony at the Pentagon Chapel. We were told that security would be very tight and that we should arrive at 11.45 a.m. sharp at the South Parking Lot Entrance, from where our group would be escorted into the building.

I arrived, parked the car and walked with the World Peace Flame toward the entrance. However, I had made a mistake—the South Entrance was at the other end of the building and I was told I would have to drive right around it to another parking lot.

The Pentagon is one of the largest buildings in the world. I now only had five minutes left before I needed to be on its other side. I ran back to the car and tried to navigate my way around the immense complex via the huge parking lots that surround it. I soon realised it is impossible to drive around the

Pentagon! I would have to exit onto the complicated junction of freeways that surround the building, circle right around and re-enter on the south side.

I found an exit ramp out of the parking lot, but as I drove down it I suddenly realised that if I continued, I would be on the freeway going the wrong way, crossing the Potomac River into Washington D.C. Now what should I do? If I continued into D.C. I would certainly miss the security check, and with it the opportunity to bring the World Peace Flame into the Pentagon. Yet if I stopped here on the exit ramp, then where would I go?

There was a big, black, official sedan behind me so I slowed down and pulled over as far as I could to let it pass. Instead, it pulled over right behind me. 'Oh no,' I thought. 'Now I am going to get a ticket from this Pentagon official for illegal driving.'

A big man in a military uniform got out of the car and walked towards me. When he reached my window, he looked in and said, 'You seem lost. How can I help you?'

'I'm sorry,' I said. 'Yes, I am lost. I'm trying to get to the South Parking Lot. I have a presentation to make at the Pentagon Chapel at noon, and I am supposed to meet my party at the South Entrance at 11.45 a.m., which is *now!*'

'Don't worry,' the man replied warmly, 'I'll get you there. As soon as these other cars go by, we'll back along this exit ramp and I'll lead you to the South Parking Lot.'

I was totally amazed! First, I wasn't getting a ticket for illegally stopping on a ramp to enter a freeway. Second, this Pentagon official was going to lead me backwards along the exit ramp (which was undoubtedly illegal), and then guide me to my destination.

I thought the Pentagon contained the 'bad guys' making preparations for war, and that we were the 'good guys' with our Peace Flames! Yet here was this military official stopping to help someone who was clearly lost, and not just pointing where to go, but actually escorting me to my destination! Now, that's peacemaking. His words and actions brought me so much relief! Within minutes, I had parked in the South Lot, run to the South Entrance, and found my group of peacemakers just as they were entering through the security check. I had made it!

When it was my turn to speak, I explained about how the air forces of the world helped to make the World Peace Flame possible. 'You see the Flame shines on everyone equally,' I said. 'It's not about 'us' versus 'them'; it's about 'we'—our common humanity.' I went on to tell the audience about my journey that morning and how a Pentagon official had so unexpectedly helped me, dropping his own agenda to aid someone in need.

For me, this is the essence of how the World Peace Flame encapsulates peacemaking: meeting the needs of those around me, asking 'How can I help?' and letting go of my own agenda in order to help someone else. I have found that when I am able to let go of my own drive and wilfulness to assist someone who needs my help, peace comes immediately to my heart. I use the World Peace Flame as a reminder of my common humanity with everyone I meet. Not only does my happiness increase as a result, I usually find that what I was trying to achieve still arrives with perfect timing.

Ned Hartfiel, USA

Success in our relationships depends on the attitude we carry into our interactions. Einstein once said that 'there are two ways to experience life. Either everything is a miracle, or nothing is a miracle.' If you can learn to build your relationships on the principle of drawing the highest out of the other person, you will soon dis-

cover a new sense of the miraculous in your life.

In your interactions with people, try to let your thoughts slow down for a moment and let go, a little, of the things you want to gain. Instead, imagine a light shining within the person in front of you—either in their heart or their mind—and ask yourself what you could do that would help draw out their highest.

Expect all sorts of wonderful outcomes from then on!

> *Now the light comes, the light that makes me one with all life.*
> *Let my life be like thy rainbow, whose colors teach us unity.*
>
> Native American Affirmation
> Central America

The Flame with a Mind of Its Own

The World Peace Flame means many things to many people. Here is Carel's philosophy, simple yet profound.

I have thought much about what a flame represents within us. A flame is a symbol reminding me of the inner light that shines within myself as well as in all human beings. In this way it is common to us all and so is the basis of unity.

Let me give you a little example.

One December my wife and I were invited to attend a mid-winter celebration near our village in the east of The Netherlands. It is a great tradition in our part of the country to light candles to celebrate the passage of mid-winter's eve and the return to longer daylight hours after the short winter days. It crossed my mind that it would be great if the World Peace Flame could be used to light the candles for the ceremony. However, in my experience bringing ideas from other organisations into celebrations like these is not always appreciated, so I let go of the thought.

The day before the celebration the phone rang. It was the organiser of the event! She said she'd heard about the idea of a Flame lit from all the continents of the world, and how wonderful it would be if the candles at the ceremony could be lit from it. If we liked the idea, she continued, we could give all the participants at the celebration a small World Peace Flame candle so they could take the 'feeling' of the experience back home with them. Perhaps, she concluded, we might even like to tell all the participants about the idea behind the Flame and the story of its beginning.

Would I be interested?

Well yes, of course I would! Her ideas were exactly what I would have proposed had I taken the trouble to ask in the first place. In my heart of hearts I knew that the Flame had not intended to be ignored on that occasion, and when it was clear that I was not going to stand up for it, it stood up for itself.

It is tempting to say that this is how things would have worked out anyway. But I have seen too many extraordinary ways in which the World Peace Flame seems to 'arrange' things so that just the right things happen to inspire and empower the largest possible number of people.

To me the World Peace Flame is a reminder of something very important—the oneness that we all share. Within this oneness, the light is perfectly capable of whispering the right things to the right heart at the right time. And so we find that we are all connected.

Imagine what the world would be like if everyone was aware of this Flame, aware of this light within, aware of this connection. There could be no wars, no exploitation, no pollution, no greed or injustice because everyone would know that by hurting someone else they would be hurting themselves.

Well, in that case, why doesn't everyone just get on with it?

Maybe I am getting impatient. The Flame will do its work in its own time and to its own schedule.

For, as I found out that December day, it knows how to stand up for itself!

Carel, The Netherlands

In our heart of hearts we usually know what decisions to make. Yet how often do our minds create different perspectives that soon take us off on other tangents? Here, Carel has shown us how he learned to trust his intuition and find a way to move beyond his previous experience and do what he felt was right.

The sun shines—not on us—but in us.

John Muir
Father of American Nature Conservation

Keepers of the Flame

Do you have a dream for your life that seems so great and vast that you have no idea how to even begin the journey towards it?

Sometimes, we simply need the reassurance that our dream is a worthy goal.

One Christmas Day, we were far from friends and family at the dinner table of two big-hearted Los Angeles film stars who seem to specialise in uniting people who care about the world. As we began to describe our work with the World Peace Flame a strange gleam of excitement kindled in the eyes of the young woman sitting opposite us. She was barely in her twenties, struggling to find her way as a singer-songwriter in a large and competitive world.

She had a dream and, as we were about to discover, had never found people who might be able to understand her vision. Now, with the Peace Flame burning on the table between us, she felt that at last she had. And so she began to tell us her story...

Several years ago, I awoke one morning feeling so rich and full that I just knew I had somehow touched my deepest spirit in the night. I had dreamed that I had walked into a huge exhibition hall. All around were booths offering all sorts of experiences in life, and I thought it was a great place to be—to start with. I shopped around trying out some of these experiences. I tried 'fame' and 'riches'—well who wouldn't? Some were in exotic locations, others were set just here in the city. After a while, I stopped. All of the things on offer seemed to lead eventually to suffering. I wanted out of there.

As soon as I had this thought I noticed a door on the far side of the expo floor. I went over, walked through and found myself in a large, quiet room. In there were some figures giving off immense power, and I realised they were the guardians of wherever I now was. I looked up and there, high above me, was an amazing light, covered with layers of gossamer fabric.

I wanted so badly to be out of that expo arena, and to reach that great light. I launched myself up towards it, tearing through the first couple of layers of fabric as I passed them. I had just reached the third layer, when I felt one of the beings from the quiet room begin to hold me back. 'Let me go on up!' I begged, and I could hear other voices from above supporting me, calling down for me to be allowed to go free.

Then, from that great being holding me back came the words that changed my life forever. 'Of course she may go on upwards,' he said, addressing whoever was above me, 'but I was rather hoping she might choose to stay. You see,' he continued, 'she is one of the Keepers of the Flame, and there are so very few of them.'

As he spoke, I knew that my dream had at last shown me my purpose for being on this Earth. I am a Keeper of the Flame, and the realisation brought a fullness and joy that I cannot attempt to describe.

I have been searching ever since. Searching for what it means to be a Keeper of the Flame. Searching for a way to make a contribution to the world that is worthy of that title. I've geared my whole life towards this, yet I've never found anyone to talk to about it. I've never really known for sure if I was doing the right thing.

Now, I know what to do. And this Flame will help me achieve my dream!

Alana, Los Angeles, USA

There is a universal truth that tells us that 'like attracts like'. In other words, when we are happy we draw happiness towards us. The converse is also true, of course, since one unhappy thought can lead to a downward spiral of unhappiness.

Henry Ford once said, 'Whether you think you can or you think you can't, you are probably right.' Test this out for yourself. Next time you have to do something—and it could be something very small—let your internal dialogue be full of creative and empowering thoughts, and watch how you draw success towards you.

Alana had filled her whole heart and mind with her search, and so it was natural that she would draw circumstances to her that would nurture and give strength to her vision.

A Stroke Patient
on a Neurology Ward

There can surely be few places where the benefits of light are more needed than on a busy hospital ward. In this setting, too, the results of working skilfully with light are often quite astonishing. This nursing student's experience illustrates how the power of visualisation brought help to her patients.

I t was my first experience of working in a hospital. I was on a neurology ward and for the first time in my life I saw people dying—a young mother who left behind a family of five children, people suffering from conditions such as meningitis, Parkinson's disease, tumours, concussion. I saw patients who might or might not get better.

Here I learned how light can make living so much more attractive. I began with my World Peace Flame. Every morning and evening I lit a flame and visualised the patients and my colleagues surrounded within a circle of light. I visualised myself being strong and achieving my learning goals.

I was looking after a patient who was recovering from a stroke. Initially he received his food through a tube. However, when he was able to go onto more solid food he refused to let anyone help him eat. Two nurses tried—and failed. He didn't appreciate them feeding him, and everything they did manage to get him to swallow soon came back up. A little later I was asked to try. Before I began, I sat down to talk with him. Before

I knew it he was talking nineteen to the dozen to me!

With this atmosphere of friendship established, he gave me permission to feed him over the next few days.

Each time, before I started, I would focus and imagine that his food was filled with light. I gave him little spoonfuls and told him how I could see him getting better every day, which he loved to hear. Within my own mind I visualised him surrounded by a circle of light, healthy and able to eat again.

Eventually, I was able to feed him a full bowl of yoghurt. When I reported this back to my colleagues their mouths dropped open in astonishment. I was immediately assigned to help and guide him right through his rehabilitation and healing process. Every day I talked to him, encouraging him and feeding him, and slowly he was able to get back onto normal, solid food. One day he told me how loving and patient I was.

On the day he was allowed to go home he thanked me especially for all the care I had given him and said he would miss me. My colleagues couldn't understand this and other successes I had with patients there. 'When you are with the patients,' they told me, 'you only need to say half a word and they do exactly what you ask of them.'

I just smiled. One day I will tell them all about my experiences with light…

A.D., Belgium

Being able to bring the benefits of light to others begins by getting to know its secrets yourself. You can harness the power of light, not just for keeping your body healthy and vital, but also for keeping your emotions buoyant, your mind clear, and your interactions full of friendship and joy.

❖   *When you want to solve a conflict or build a good working relationship with a colleague, visualise them surrounded by light. Try the same with your partner, children or parents.*

❖   *If you feel vulnerable to other people's negative emotions, visualise yourself surrounded by a cloak or 'armour' of brightly shining light.*

❖   *If you need to heal part of your body, sit with the World Peace Flame and imagine its warm light filling the affected region with radiant health.*

If you are more of a feeling/kinaesthetic person than a visual person, you may find these practices are easier if you 'feel' a warm glow inside and around you.

Try doing this for a week at least, before you judge your results. And then write and tell us your successes!

The Lighter Side of Life

It is one thing to experience a sense of inner knowing and right-ness that helps you find your way through life. It is quite another to discover that you can make a personal relationship with this higher part of yourself. Here, as Rika discovers, light can become a doorway into a relationship with the best friend you could ever have. Yet, in order to begin the relationship, you have to start the dialogue. Here you will read one way to begin a 'conversation with God'.

L ight has always been important to me, whether it is in the form of the starry night sky, the sun or fire. As a kid grow-ing up in Belgium I was so fascinated by the stars, the planets and in particular the sun that I wanted to become an astronomer. (My ambition faded when Dad told me that I would have to be really good at maths!) There was something about light that beckoned me, that touched me on a level I was not conscious of. Somehow, it made me feel connected with a higher part of myself.

As I grew up, that feeling gradually got buried under tons of other experiences, ambitions and wishes. On the surface I had everything that should have given me all the joy in the world: a caring boyfriend, a beautiful loft of my own and a well-paid job as an architect. But inside I felt restless and dis-satisfied with myself and my life as a whole. I knew that there had to be more to life than having a designer fridge!

I was twenty-seven when my world turned upside down.

My boyfriend and I broke up and I hit a brick wall. While people saw me on the outside as a pretty cool, together young woman who knew what she wanted, I had to face some different facts. On the inside I was thoroughly unhappy, couldn't keep a relationship going and was pretty self-centred because I was looking for happiness outside myself. I didn't want to stay like this.

I cried many nights. Perhaps my tears of desperation were my prayer, because the answer came in the form of a friend.

In 1999 I was present with many others during the lighting ceremony of the World Peace Flame in Wales. During this particular Life Conference I met a friend I really trusted. He had all the qualities I wanted in my life—compassion, happiness, leadership, sincerity and the ability to inspire lots of people.

I wanted to know his secret. Whatever he had, I wanted it!

He recommended I get a candle. 'Sit with this light as you start the day and again at the end of your day,' he said. 'Talk to it and it will help you find the happiness you are looking for.'

He suggested that sitting with a light outside yourself helps you connect with the inner flame… As without, so within.

His advice was a completely new concept to me. I had been brought up to think that trees, rivers, the sea and the stars are just 'objects'—in fact, that the whole of creation is merely mechanical—and at first I couldn't easily accept the idea of talking to a flame as if it were alive. Nevertheless, I decided to go ahead and give it a try.

In the beginning I felt really silly talking to that flame. However, after a while the awkwardness faded and I began to feel that within the light of the flame was a friend I could relate to. Gradually, I caught myself looking forward to my evening talks with my little-friend-the-flame. Whatever my problem, he listened unconditionally. If I felt fed up with something, or jealous, or whatever, I would stare at the flame and tell him my problem. Then I would sit quietly, focus on my heart and listen. It took me a while to get the hang of still-ing my mind, and for a long time nothing seemed to happen.

Then, one night when I was sitting in meditation in front of my light, I heard a question inside: 'This is better than email, isn't it?!'

My jaw dropped open in astonishment and I looked at my chest, for the question had come directly from my heart, *not* my head. I laughed with enjoyment and amazement. It was the beginning of a conversation that has since become the most precious thing in my life.

I started to review my day with the flame and wrote every-thing down. Together we agreed on where I could have been a bit more selfless or a bit less angry or judgemental. We would have dialogues together. I would say something like, 'I'm feeling so jealous at the moment,' and my new friend would respond, 'Oh, so we're jealous are we?' and then go on to explain why I felt that way and what I could do to over-come it.

Slowly I started to realise that through my little friend I was connecting with the innermost part of me that 'knows', the part that watches whatever the situation is, the part that seems eternal and doesn't get entangled in emotions. I began to notice two streams of consciousness within me; one that took my mind into the daily world of being 'busy' and another that took me to a realm of truth inside that gave me an eagle's per-spective on my day. All the emotional ups and downs would drop away as I stepped into this world of friendship and fun. It was like talking to my highest self, the part of me that is real.

In the evening I made a habit of telling the flame my plans for the next day. I began to realise that every word I was say-ing to my friend was being heard. It wasn't always easy to take on his advice! Yet when I did, miracles would happen. One freezing cold winter night I distinctly heard, 'Wouldn't it be great to go for a walk before dawn tomorrow?' I didn't think so! Nevertheless, there I was at six o'clock the next morning in the freezing fields outside my house wondering what on earth I was doing. Suddenly, I looked up and twenty-four shooting stars showered past me, one after the other. I was left gasping for breath at the beauty of it all, recalling my starry-night fascination as a kid.

The flame wasn't just helping me out. My sister was once desperately looking for a new job. I said, 'Look, this is how the universe works. You have to tell it what you want, so it can deliver the goods. Make a list of how you see the job you'd like to have, what you'd like to be doing, how your relationships would be with the people there, and then read it out to the light every night.' Within months she had found her dream job. And then, six months later, she got married, her new boss supporting her as best woman!

My little friend the flame became the most precious gift anybody could have given to me. My whole perspective on life turned upside down, and as a result, so did my life. (Yes, we do create our own reality through the power of our own mind!) I knew exactly what to do and where to go. I wanted to work with people who lived with the same fun and compassion as I had seen in my friend that day at the conference. I didn't want to live for myself any more; I wanted to start living for others. Looking back, I realise that the more you connect with a flame—which shines equally on all—the more you want to help others and the lighter you feel.

I left for Wales to join the Life Foundation and when the friend who had given me the advice to sit with the flame saw me arrive, he just smiled and nodded.

I believe the aim of every soul on this planet is to come home, and to realise its sense of belonging. I know that the World Peace Flame has the power to help us do that. I realise these words will stay empty unless you make the light your own. A wise person once said that if something touches you it is an invitation to put it into practice... all you need is trust!

Now, nearly four years later, I can honestly say my life is

totally changed, on the outside as well as on the inside! At this very moment, I'm designing the World Peace Flame monument in North Wales... talk about miracles...

Rika, North Wales

Happiness is a state of being that flows out of gratitude for what you already have.

Rika's Flame

Did You Get What You Asked For?

All great quests for truth should be accompanied by exquisite moments of hilarity. Carrying the World Peace Flame will certainly do this for you! And, as Pam discovers in this story, you might find that life has more to give you than you thought.

One day I set off to walk from my home at the Life Foundation's centre in the Nant Ffrancon Valley, Snowdonia, to visit friends on a neighbouring mountain. A friend joined me; we were both in our late sixties, and glad to have each other's company on our walk into the mountains. With us we carried my World Peace Flame lantern.

We tramped across the fields and passed through the forest at the end of the valley. Eventually we came to the bridge that crosses the road leading up the mountain. Just as we arrived there, an extra gust of wind whipped around us and playfully tugged at our clothes. When I looked down, my Flame had gone out!

It was raining and all my matches had got soaked, so I said to my friend, 'I think we'll have to knock on the door of this cottage here and ask them for a light.'

'I'll do that,' my friend replied brightly, and trotted off to the cottage.

Soon he was back, looking perplexed. 'A man answered the door and when I asked him for a light, this is what he gave me. I couldn't seem to make him understand that this wasn't what we needed.'

In his hands he held an electric light bulb.

We laughed and laughed. All we'd needed was a match, but out of the goodness of his heart this man had given us much more than we'd asked for. We carried his light bulb like a royal trophy up to our friends' house!

Pam, North Wales

Have you ever been given something unexpected that you didn't need at all? Those moments can give you immeasurable happiness if you simply accept the gift in the spirit in which it was meant.

It might surprise you to discover the size of the gifts life has in store for you.

At the European Parliament

A close friend of ours has more than twenty-five years' experience in international politics—fifteen as a Member of the European Parliament—and so is intimately familiar with the corridors and meeting rooms of the centre of European decision making. Here, she describes a series of events that just should not have been possible under normal circumstances...

The World Peace Flame is being presented to many of the world's decision makers, and so some time ago Savitri asked me if I would organise a visit of the Flame to the European Parliament.

We started the day in a meeting with a former colleague and friend from Ireland, leader of one of the political parties in the European Parliament. A few years earlier he had organised a memorable trip to Auschwitz, where we had lit candles and talked with people who had been interned there during the war.

He was very much impressed by the World Peace Flame and Andrew, Savitri and I had a warm meeting with him.

And then, as we walked through the European Parliament after the meeting, with Savitri carrying the World Peace Flame, strange and wonderful things began to happen...

It felt as if people were attracted by the Flame. Somehow we just happened to 'bump into' a great many leading national and European politicians as we were walking through the

Parliament buildings on our way out…

I have been in politics for twenty-five years, and I have never in my life witnessed anything like this day.

Why were all those people in Parliament on that one particular day? They are not normally in Brussels, certainly not at the same time, and certainly not all within the corridors and meeting rooms of the Parliament buildings.

The President of the European Parliament at the time, who is usually abroad or ensconced in meeting rooms, happened to walk by us, surrounded by civil servants. When she saw us she broke out of her group to speak with us. She accepted a World Peace Flame as a gift which is now in her office.

We met the United Nations' Commissioner for Human Rights who listened, impressed, as we presented the Peace Flame and described its history.

At the bottom of a flight of stairs we met the Vice-President of the Parliament. He also received a Flame with interest. Outside another meeting room we met politicians from Denmark, Belgium and Germany. All were intrigued by the history of the Flame and appreciated receiving it as a gift.

And so it went on, quite literally for hours and hours.

Altogether the World Peace Flame was accepted by over twenty people from governments, national parliaments and from the European Parliament. Half of them were leaders or in the senior leadership of Europe's main political parties and institutions.

Our experience on this day should not have been possible. To arrange to meet all these dignitaries I would normally have needed six months of organisation, sending emails, writing letters, making phone calls… We would have had to go to Paris, Washington, Berlin, London, Geneva and many other places.

I hadn't made any of the arrangements that should have been necessary in order to meet these people. All I had done was set up just one meeting with a Member of Parliament from a small country.

My friends in Parliament hardly believe my account of the story.

How was it all possible?

The day has been another illustration for me of the immense potential of the World Peace Flame.

J.L., The Netherlands

In the last decade or so, many branches of science have begun to recognise that everything in life is connected.

In disciplines from quantum physics to psychology we find that there is no such thing as an objective experiment—the subject and experimenter are intimately connected. In ecology, economics and organisational development we are discovering through Complexity Theory that a small change in one part of a system can precipitate massive changes across the whole.

And at a very personal level, we as human beings are beginning to realise that as we change our individual perceptions, motivations and actions, we affect the way others respond to us. This in turn affects the way these people behave to others... and so on in a wave that can extend indefinitely through society. This effect may even happen directly at a level of conscious awareness or emotionality. When Mozart played the piano, the whole opera house was transfixed. A landmark national sporting achievement can change the atmosphere of a whole country. Or a disaster can leave a whole nation's people mourning.

Sometimes it is possible for many factors like these to come together all at once and shape apparently unconnected events into perfect patterns of natural flow and synchronicity—such as we experienced that day at the European Parliament. We can only begin to explain these remarkable occurrences when we seek to understand the larger patterns of transformation across society.

In many respects, the development of the World Peace Flame as it spreads across the earth is a cutting-edge example of how human emotionality, perceptions and pure intent can create a positive influence across the whole of our society.

Journey of a Sacred Flame

This ancient legend from Italy is one of the world's great allegories of the spiritual path—or indeed any journey to success. It is a longer story, like all good adventures, and will take a little longer to study than the other stories in this book. Yet it will give you all the guiding principles you need for attaining your goal, whatever that might be. See if you can discover them during your journey with Raniero. Bon voyage!

M any, many years ago, a young and adventurous man named Raniero di Raniero lived in the city of Florence. Son of an armourer, he was so strong that he could win any fight or gain any trophy he cared to try for.

Raniero was the bravest man who had ever lived in Florence, but he was also the proudest. He was loud-mouthed and boastful, cruel to animals and quick to pick a fight.

The love of his life was a young woman named Francesca. Francesca adored Raniero too and determined to marry him, even in the face of her father's protestations. Eventually, her father gave his consent, but only after exacting a promise from the young Raniero that if ever Francesca should find life with him so hard that she wanted to return to her family, he would not prevent her from doing so.

In the pride and confidence of youth the two readily agreed and happily began to plan their wedding.

Not long after their marriage, Raniero decided he would take up marksmanship. He soon became so skilled that he no longer found it challenging to aim at a stationary target and began to set his sights on something more difficult. He asked a page to open the door of the cage where Francesca's favourite quail was sitting and shot it as it fluttered into the air.

When Francesca learned what he had done she was distraught. However, she reasoned that his act was not a big thing in proportion to her love for him, and so she soon forgave him.

As time went by, Raniero's exploits increasingly involved him in activities that were hurtful to Francesca. He humiliated her father, her brother, and her family's name. Each time she tried to forgive him, but gradually she found it more and more difficult. She had always thought that her love for him was indestructible but, to her alarm, she found that it was slowly but surely being worn away.

Eventually she decided to leave Raniero and go back to her family before her love for him was completely destroyed.

Raniero was devastated by the loss. However, there was no way he could force her back; his promise to her father could not be gainsaid. Knowing her great love for him, he decided he would attempt to win her back.

He went out and pursued some robbers who had been terrorising the people of Florence and brought them to justice. He became a soldier, a commander and finally was knighted by the Emperor. Yet none of his successes was enough to bring his beloved Francesca back.

At the time, the Church was seeking to enlist support for the Crusades, and Raniero decided he had no other option than to try to find renown on the battlefield of the Holy Land.

Before departing Florence, he made a promise in front of the Madonna in the Cathedral that he would offer back to her everything he gained in battle.

**** **** ****

Raniero excelled himself in the battles. He was first over the ramparts of Jerusalem and was later publicly honoured for his bravery.

When the city had been safely captured, and all the murder and plunder completed, the warriors put on penitents' cloaks and entered the Church of the Holy Sepulchre, the holiest of holies in Christendom, the place where Jesus arose from the Tomb.

As a reward for his bravery Raniero was allowed to be the first to light his candle from the lights burning before Christ's sacred Sepulchre. Puffed up with pride, Raniero took care to keep his candle alight throughout the rest of the day.

Later that night there was great revelry in Raniero's tent. He had won every victory and felt sure his successes would at last win favour with his beloved Francesca.

Towards the end of the night, a great argument broke out amongst the men about who had won the greatest trophy of the day. Finally, with much merriment, the assembly pointed at the candle still burning at Raniero's side. 'We have won gold and jewels and a city of treasure, but none of us has a prize to match that of the great warrior here,' they guffawed. 'Yet he will never be able to take this richest of gifts back to his Madonna, nor will he ever win back the heart of his Lady.' And they fell over each other in merriment.

It was too much for Raniero. He drew himself up and roared at the assembly, 'If you cowards think that I am the sort of man who leaves my vows unfulfilled then leave this place! I need no help from the likes of you. Tomorrow I shall prove that Raniero di Raniero will accomplish his vow and win the heart of his beloved!' And with that he stalked out of the assembly carrying his candle.

The next morning, Raniero set out on his journey. Somehow he would have to travel alone all the way to Florence carrying a lighted candle. It had never been done before, but Raniero di Raniero was not to be deterred. He would accomplish his feat.

He started his journey in full armour, cloaked in pilgrim's wear, carrying his sword and battle club along with a supply of wax candles attached to his saddle. He started slowly, shielding the light with his cloak, but soon his horse began to quicken its pace and no matter how carefully he tried to shield the flame from the wind, it was in danger of going out. The only way he could think of protecting the precious flame was to turn round and sit backwards on the horse so his body would shield it from the wind.

It wasn't long before he was attacked by robbers. Twelve men surrounded him, brandishing swords. He saw instantly that he could easily fight his way past them, yet what then of his flame? His only chance was to avoid a fight, so he said to them, 'I am under holy oath to keep this flame burning, so you may take whatever you want from me. I won't resist at all, so long as you promise to leave me with these wax candles and the flame.'

The robbers had been looking nervously at the obvious might of this proud warrior and were immediately relieved by his offer. They greedily took everything except his candle, but in the last had pity on him. One of them left behind a decrepit old horse for him to continue his journey.

Raniero was beginning to seriously doubt the wisdom of his journey. Yet something within him had begun to awaken. A yearning to complete his mission seized him. It was so great it seemed to fill his whole soul. He would continue on his way.

Before long he was travelling through a dry and barren land, where he met a goatherd. The Christians had robbed the man of virtually every animal he possessed and so he immediately set upon Raniero with his staff. Raniero could offer no resistance while he was carrying his flame, and the goatherd soon became ashamed of his actions. He began to lead Raniero's horse along the road. 'He must think I am a holy man,' thought Raniero, as his journey continued.

That night he stopped at a market town, settling down for

the night beside his horse and some piles of hay, intending to stay awake all night. He was so tired, however, that he fell asleep almost immediately, awaking the next morning greatly refreshed—but his flame was nowhere to be seen. 'Someone has taken it away and put it out,' he thought disconsolately.

Just then his host came up to him with the candle. 'I could see this was important to you, sir, so I took it from where you were sleeping in case you knocked it over, and have kept it alight all night for you. Go in peace now.'

Raniero beamed at him and continued on his way.

Living only on the alms of pilgrims, who were by now flocking in large numbers to Jerusalem, he travelled northward and commenced the long journey to Florence. All along the route he guarded the candle, never at ease for a moment. The slightest breeze or one raindrop could mean the end of his quest.

His journey took him over a high mountain, where a mighty storm came upon him. He sheltered for two days and nights in a cave up in the hills while snow and freezing winds swirled all around. However, he regarded his flame as very sacred and did not want to take a light from it to kindle an ordinary fire, even to save his own life. Just when he began to feel certain he would freeze to death a mighty thunderbolt struck a bush in front of the cave and it burst into flames. He was able to warm himself by a fire without disturbing his candle flame.

As he continued his journey he began to understand his life more deeply. He thought of Francesca, and how she had tried to guard her love for him in much the same way that he now guarded this light. He realised for the first time what he had done to her, and that it would not be by force of arms that he would regain her heart.

One day he fell asleep with the candle propped up beside him. While he slept it began to rain. He awoke with a start many hours later, fearful that his flame must have been extinguished by the rain. To his amazement, it was still burning strongly. Two small birds were hovering above it, protecting it from the rain with their wings. Raniero was thoughtful. The birds must have recognised that his only desire was now to protect this fragile flame in front of him and they were safe in his presence.

Another time, he was approached by a woman living in a remote valley. 'My fire has gone out and I can't cook anything for my children to eat. They are famished!' she called. 'Please give me a light from your candle.' Unable to bear the thought of leaving her children to suffer he used his sacred flame to rekindle her fire. Soon afterwards, as he approached a town in the pouring rain, a peasant took pity on him and threw a cloak over him. The cloak fell on the candle and extinguished it! Almost beside himself with grief, he suddenly remembered the woman by the hut and rode back to rekindle his light from the fire he had given her.

Gradually, he neared the end of his journey. As he rode close to Florence, he thought back to his time in the Holy Land. He thought of the battles he had won and the trophies he had gained. Soon he would be back there to accrue more honour for Christendom and, of course, himself. Yet he noticed that this prospect did not fill him with excitement as it once would have done. On the contrary, it filled him with repulsion. He realised that the Raniero that was returning from the conquests in the Holy Land was a very different man from the one who had departed from Florence all that time ago.

As he entered Florence and its thronged streets the people saw only a madman dressed in rags and carrying a candle. They tried to put out the candle and so Raniero held it high above him as he rode along. This only excited them more, and soon the whole street was full of people leaping about trying to extinguish his sacred flame. Just as his path took him under a balcony, a woman standing there plucked the flame from his hands and ran inside with it. It was Francesca.

As soon as he lost the flame he fell from his horse, senseless. The street immediately emptied, as no-one wanted to bother with an injured madman. Only Francesca stayed. She brought the flame down to him, and as soon as its light touched his face he awoke. 'Please show me the way to the Cathedral,' he whispered.

Francesca had recognised Raniero immediately, but his gaze was fixed so single-mindedly on the flame that he hardly noticed her. On these last few steps of his journey nothing was going to distract him from his sacred flame.

Francesca led Raniero into the Cathedral. It was Easter Saturday, and all the candles on the High Altar lay waiting to be lit in celebration of the resurrection the next day.

The priest announced to all who were gathered that Raniero di Raniero had returned from Jerusalem carrying a Sacred Fire, and if more great lights were brought to Florence, it would surely rise to be the greatest city on earth! For a few moments Francesca was overjoyed, but as Raniero was led up to the altar by the Bishop, an old man stood and blocked the way.

It was the father of one of the many young men Raniero had worsted in his early days. 'This is a very fine accomplishment, no doubt,' he said, 'and I feel sure that such a great knight as Raniero will now prove to us that he has kept this flame alight throughout the entire journey.' He looked witheringly at Raniero.

The seed of doubt had been sown. Of course, there was no way he could prove his claim. The people rushed to support one side or the other, and Raniero began to give up all hope he would be believed. Once such a doubt has been planted it will destroy truth faster than the rain falls from heaven. Raniero began to think his light was already extinguished. Looking pale and haggard, he held it high above his head.

Just at that moment, a little bird flew into the church. Confused and disoriented by all the commotion below, it flew straight into the candle, extinguishing it. Yet the little bird continued flying. Soon it was evident that its feathers had caught fire. For a moment it fluttered around the high arches of the chancel, just like a flickering flame, then it swooped down across the altar, lighting a candle on the Madonna's Shrine as it passed. Quickly, Raniero reached up and caught the bird in mid flight. Holding it gently within the folds of his cloak, he extinguished the flames.

'It is God's will! God has spoken!' cried the Bishop, raising his staff.

'It is God's will!' echoed all the people, enraptured by the miracle that had taken place in front of their eyes.

Raniero had reached his goal.

The sacred fire had arrived at the Altar of the Madonna and his long and marvellous journey was now complete.

Story retold by Andrew Wells

Once we pick up the Flame of Hope and set foot upon our journey, we begin a path to success well-mapped by the ancient traditions. Raniero's story of self-transformation is our own, if we choose to have the courage and clarity of conviction to propel us towards our goal.

What lessons can Raniero's adventures teach us? Here is an eleven-point course in success-making that will show you how to harness your inner strength and take you towards your highest goals.

1. *Raniero began his journey with all his weapons and power. He started off relying on his status and role. It was not to last. Ask yourself what roles and status symbols you rely on for happiness. Do they really bring you what you want?*

2. *Before long, Raniero's flame started to go out. He paused and took some space for reflection—as should we all when we encounter adversity—and used his creativity to discern a solution.*

3. *Then he made the decision not to fight—for the first time stepping outside of his status, role and livelihood. As a result, everything was taken—except the things he really needed. Life will always give you what you need. Always.*

4. *As a result of this first act of commitment, Raniero's goal was now fully awakened in him. Frequently, we do not ascend to the full power of our convictions until we test them at least once in the fire of adversity. For your journey to be successful, choose not to shy away from obstacles. They will give you the power to succeed.*

5. *Then his host in the market town kept his candle alight all night. Once this power is awakened, you will receive help in all sorts of ways you never expected. Similarly the lightning and the two birds brought help as a result of the power of his convictions.*

6. *Raniero then began to examine his life. As the unnecessary clutter was removed and his convictions tested, he began to know himself and his purpose more clearly. He realised he had been trying to reach his goal—regaining Francesca—using the wrong methods! Ask yourself if your life is trying to tell you to do things differently. Listen with honesty and faith, in the certainty that life will always help you achieve the dreams that are in harmony with your essential nature.*

7. *The woman came to ask him for his light. Now Raniero makes another huge leap. Instead of receiving help from life, he begins to give it. As a result, he is saved from*

calamity when the villager's cloak extinguishes the flame. As Saint Francis said, 'It is in giving that we receive.' A journey towards our goal cannot succeed unless we give back to the spiral of life.

8. *En route to Florence, Raniero realised he had changed. In discovering new parts of himself he had lost interest in his old ways of living. When you are growing and transforming, remember that it's okay to let go of the old. As you do, great new horizons will open up ahead of you.*

9. *By the time he reached the City, Raniero had developed such singleness of purpose he didn't even recognise Francesca. That total focus pulled him to his ultimate goal.*

10. *The final challenge Raniero faced was doubt. More powerful than the winds and the snow, stronger than robbers, temptations, hunger and thirst, doubt is the ultimate threat to your journey. Never entertain a doubt or help create one in others. Instead, stay focused on your goal. If you feel a doubt entering your heart, take yourself back to a time when you felt certainty and think of all the good reasons you had then for your conviction. Try writing them down, perhaps several times over twenty-four hours. When you focus on your original assurance, you will more easily recognise what is doubt and what is truth.*

11. *Finally, Raniero was saved by a miracle. His success did not come from pride, ego or self expression. He gave his all to his goal, and a power far beyond himself eventually enabled him to complete his journey. Raniero's greatest lesson to us is that when we give our all to a goal that is free of selfishness we gain help from forces far, far greater than ourselves.*

HEALING ~ OVERCOMING TRAGEDY

" *At times our own light goes out and is rekindled by a spark from another person. Each of us has cause to think with deep gratitude of those who have lit the flame within us...* "

Albert Schweitzer

A Flame for Auschwitz

Our fundamental beliefs about ourselves, our purpose, and the nature of our world form the essential foundations of our existence. And sometimes it is important that these beliefs are shaken to the core. How else can we truly choose the foundations of our life, and know for certain that we are building our life on aspirations that are innately our own?

Read how an experience like this transformed a young woman's life forever.

My brother does a lot of caring work and has often told me about the strength you can gain by looking quietly into a candle flame. I never really paid much attention to him until one evening when I was about twenty-three.

I had just moved to Melbourne, Australia, and was revelling in the discovery of an exciting new group of friends. We would have all sorts of fun together, and on this particular evening had planned a night at the cinema to see *Schindler's List*. I didn't know much about its story and I expected a great evening in the company of great people.

Instead, I received a terrible shock.

Nothing in my life had prepared me for what I experienced during that film. I watched aghast as the atrocities of Birkenau and Auschwitz unfolded in front of my eyes. I had heard of the Holocaust—who hasn't—but somehow growing up in Australia forty years later I never fully grasped what it really meant. I didn't know that as many as six million people were killed under the cruellest of circumstances. I knew that the Nazis had persecuted the Jews, but to actually see the systematic way in which they set out to murder a whole culture was horrific. I didn't know that people could be so calculating, so cold and so hateful.

At the end of the movie I didn't go out with my friends. I went home. I was blinded by the experience. How could human beings do that to each other? I didn't know whether I was numbed by anger or numbed by depression. How could that degree of cruelty be a part of humanity? Was the same cruelty lying within me? What about all the good I thought the human race was capable of? Was it all a mirage? The questions raged through my mind, piling numbness upon numbness as each new thought struck home.

I was shattered, my faith in humanity in tatters. I didn't know what to do.

I sat in my little apartment, alone and numb, unable to think of anything except humanity's chilling cruelty. I was frozen and in despair.

And then, I heard a question inside. 'What would my brother do in this situation?' The small voice answered itself. 'He would go and light a candle.'

It seemed a good idea. There was little else worth doing in the stark, cruel world I had just been propelled into. Moving like an automaton I went upstairs, pulled out a small candle, placed it on a table and sat back in an easy chair, gazing blankly at it. It was a tiny speck of gold in a room grown cold and dark.

For quite a long time, nothing happened. I just sat staring dully at the candle. And then slowly I began to feel a calming peace spread throughout my mind and body. The warm gold of the flame began to absorb my attention. I found my thoughts wandering to people I knew who were working for peace or helping others. I thought of my parents who always tried to help the people around them and of my other brother who is the kindest man I've ever met. Gradually, I found that the light of the flame began to penetrate my mind so deeply it felt as if it was being absorbed by the very cells of my body.

As it did so, a new perspective began to dawn. I knew that people were often afraid. Did cruelty in humanity come from a reaction to fear of the unknown, or to a fear of difference? Was great cruelty simply a reaction to great fear? If so, then what about humanity's other reactions? What about how we respond to 'learning', to 'understanding' or to 'peace and goodness'? My thoughts began to change. As well as being the greatest destroyers on the earth, we could also be the greatest healers. We could, when we chose, bring unparalleled benefit to the world around us.

The flame had begun to speak to me. I found myself caught up in its light, a wave of exultation engulfing me. Yes! There was a way forward. Humanity was capable of the highest good and our task in life was to try to make that possible. I was filled with excitement.

Now, finally, I was able to lift my gaze up and away from the flame. I looked around in awe at the potential life could offer. Although I was alone in a darkened room, I saw a rich texture of possibilities and choice all around me.

That evening I grew up a lot. I realised humanity has a choice between cruelty and goodness. The path we take is literally only a choice away. And I knew that night that I had made my decision. I would choose goodness, and help others do the same.

My experience with the light had set me free.

F.W., Australia

Mansukh's mother always said that the stars have many lessons to teach us that can only be learned through the darkness of the night. She said, 'Whenever you feel you are in the dark night of the soul, do not forget to sit and listen to the message that is being given to you. What is it that is trying to awaken in you?'

> *A diamond must be cut before its light can shine out.*
> *The discovering of error is the uncovering of the light.*
> *Blessed is he who sees the star of his soul as the light that is seen in the port from the sea...*
> *In the light I behold Thy beauty, beloved; through the darkness, thy mystery is revealed to my heart.*

Hazrat Inayat Khan

Baptism of Sunlight

This young nursing student's ability to visualise light and utilise the power of sunlight enabled her to create an amazing rapport with patients.

As a trainee nurse you experience a lot. You find yourself encountering many things you could never even have imagined.

My baptism of fire in the nursing profession was my first period of practical work, which was at a nursing home close to my village.

The patients were all in need of a lot of care as they were bedridden or no longer capable of taking care of themselves. Essentially, they had come to this place to die. Most of the residents spent the entire day sitting in wheelchairs, and the highlights of their life consisted of being taken out of bed, being washed and eating at the three set times of the day. That was all. Helping them with their physical difficulties was hard enough for me, but the way so many of them had nothing to do, nowhere to go and no-one to care for them was almost unbearable. I often found myself wondering why on earth I had chosen this work and just what it was that kept me going amidst all the challenges I faced.

I had the advantage of doing my training there in the spring. The sun shone nearly every day. One day I asked some of the old people if they ever went outside. They all said no, some saying they had not been out for months.

It was all up to me. I could smoke a cigarette with them in the living room or take them out into the garden. Not much of a choice, was it? We all have a deep need to feel the vitalising force of sunlight radiating onto our bodies. The patients looked at me with longing in their eyes and as soon as I had taken one of them out, they all wanted to go. They all gained from the experience, some of them becoming so transformed and joyful that the regular staff could hardly believe the results.

One day I brought an elderly man back inside after being out in the sun and as I turned to go he caught my hand for a few moments. He just looked at me, without a word, tears of gratitude in his eyes. It was all the thanks I needed.

Witness the power of the sun!

The regular staff had not thought of taking these people outside. I wonder about this every now and then. Why don't we stop more often to think of the power of the sun and light? They are so important for our well-being and happiness!

A.D., Belgium

Could light be the medicine of the future? If you were to look for a broad-spectrum medicine that could assist a wide variety of mind-body related illnesses, was essentially free from side effects and involved no intrusive substances, it would be hard to find anything better than light!

As you can read in the section on 'Why Light?' adequate exposure to full-spectrum, natural light helps the body create vitamin D as well as balancing night and day time rhythms. People living in more northerly or southerly latitudes, or who spend most of their lives under artificial lights, can significantly improve their health and well-being by making time to be in natural light.

For your own daily light therapy programme, make a point of spending at least twenty minutes outside without wearing glasses. Feel and visualise that you are absorbing the sunlight into your body through your eyes and through your skin. Do not try to look directly at the sun—just being outside in the daylight hours is sufficient. Remember that even on a cloudy day the sun is still there behind the clouds and will benefit you.

After My Son Died

We need never be alone on our journey through life. Even when it seems our worst fears have been realised, each of us carries an innate wisdom that can bring out strengths we never knew we had. Marlies has walked this path. Here she describes the great healing that lightened her time of darkness.

I think I have always known that my son, Tycho, would die young.

When he was twelve, we planted a chestnut tree together and as soon as we had finished he stood up and said, 'I will live on in this tree after I have died.' At the time I thought it was merely one of those strange statements you hear from children from time to time, but as the months went by, this and other incidents began to weave a larger picture in my heart. At a certain moment, a deep knowing within me began to whisper that his time was coming. And then a few months later waves of grief and pain began to rise from nowhere and I knew it must be very near.

Yet, of course, a large part of me refused to think anything of these perceptions. Tycho was fourteen, the most popular boy in his class, sensitive, kind and loved by everyone. His classmates would go to him whenever they had problems. He was always supporting people, always finding ways to help them, always the most popular friend to be around. I think everybody loved him deeply. He was that sort of boy.

And then, on 16th December, I received the news that made my world stop turning. Two policemen stood at my front door and told me Tycho had drowned in our village swimming pool.

I couldn't think. I couldn't feel. 'No, it can't be possible!' was all that would come to my mind. 'He is the best swimmer and diver in the school,' my thoughts raced on. 'They must have the wrong name. It can't be him!'

But there was no denying the sincerity and concern on the policemen's faces.

They took me to the hospital where I was ushered into his room. He was lying so peacefully that the same part of my mind rushed on in reassurance, 'Oh, they've got it wrong. He's just asleep. He'll wake up soon.'

Yet the part of me that is real knew it wasn't so. He was cold, so very cold. He had been dead for two hours and slowly I began to accept the reality. My son had died.

With this realisation, an overwhelming urge to have him surrounded with light arose within me. 'Please,' I asked one of the nurses, 'do you have any candles?' She readily brought some, and soon I had placed a beautiful circle of light all around his body. Not long after this my friends Trudy and Hetty arrived to support me, bringing a World Peace Flame candle with them. As soon as I saw it I knew I should put it on Tycho's heart. With great care, I placed it right in the middle of his chest, creating a warm glow that would give light to his soul, I felt, and help him make his journey in peace.

I suppose it was with that thought that acceptance finally set in. Tycho would not be waking up again.

When my husband finally arrived—he had been in Brussels on business—we talked about what would happen next. We both felt a strong desire to have Tycho home with us until his funeral, and what followed were some of the most bitter-sweet healing moments I have ever experienced. Amidst all the pain, we found ourselves immersed in exquisite light.

Once Tycho was brought into our living room, we placed

candles all around him, with the World Peace Flame still above his heart. Almost immediately we were struck by the feeling of warmth and stillness that filled the room. Soon, it was obvious that everyone felt the same. For the next five days a constant stream of friends—adults and children—visited our house to say goodbye to Tycho. Most would stay with him for several hours, and the room always had people in it—his classmates writing letters to him, children drawing, others sitting praying or quietly talking to him. To look at him, surrounded by his sea of lights with his friends in the background was like looking into a well of peacefulness and light. It was so healing.

Every time I went near Tycho I intuitively felt I should massage the soles of his feet. I did this for five days. For all that time his soles remained very soft and I had the feeling that I was helping his soul leave his body to continue on its journey.

On the day before Tycho's funeral one of his best friends, a Moslem refugee from Bosnia, took out his prayer rosary and whispered, 'Can I give it to Tycho?' I knew it meant the world to him. I watched while this fourteen-year-old boy approached his best friend and carefully laid his most treasured possession across his hands. He had wanted to give Tycho something he could take with him, he told me afterwards, and the best thing he could think of was the rosary he had used every day in prayer for years. Where does such wisdom come from?

The day before the funeral, I gave all Tycho's classmates a candle, which they lit from the World Peace Flame candle resting upon his heart. 'You can use these whenever you want to remember Tycho,' I said. They stood around him during the funeral itself, a sea of brightly lit faces flickering in love as they said their last goodbyes to their friend. Even now, two years later, many of them still light these candles whenever they want to think of Tycho.

So, my son had now been laid to rest. Yet, how was I to find respite from the aching void that remained within me?

Gradually, the same inner knowing that had heralded my son's passing now began to guide my healing.

Above all, I knew I must not deny or bury my pain. I began to use all my knowledge as a Dru Yoga teacher upon myself. I used yoga and meditation and spent long, long periods within the healing forces of nature. I kept the World Peace Flame burning by me and found comfort gazing into its warm glow. Whereas in the past I had sent my prayers for peace out into the world, now its light supported me.

Healing comes in parts, I have found. In my classes and consultations, each time I found a way to sincerely help someone else I noticed that the pain subsided a little. I travelled to Ground Zero in New York, and Tuzla in Bosnia, where I found further healing by lighting World Peace Flames and bringing light back into these places of great suffering and darkness.

Eventually, I knew I was ready to complete my letting go. I decided to go on a pilgrimage with the World Peace Flame. For a thousand years, pilgrims have walked to Santiago de Compostella in Spain. I decided I would follow in their footsteps. I started in the south of France and walked for 900 kilometres to Santiago.

I took a stone from the base of Tycho's chestnut tree, put it in my rucksack and, with the blessings of my husband and Tycho's younger brother, set out alone on the journey. My stone represented my grief, my pain, and my son. Halfway to Santiago I would leave it on Cruz de Ferro, the highest point on the pilgrimage route, following the example of countless pilgrims before me.

Every evening I would spend time with my World Peace Flame candle, asking for help to let go of the grief I felt. During each day's walk, I would practise letting go by picking up a rock, carrying it with me for the day and then depositing it on one of the many small cairns of rocks that have been made by other pilgrims along the path.

Each day, I felt my strength returning.

One night, I was suddenly woken in the hostel I was staying at by the sounds of Marco, a German pilgrim, who had been struck by a very severe asthma attack. We rushed to his side as he crawled out of bed, writhing in panic and calling for an ambulance. None of us knew any Spanish, and in our remote location we had no way of calling medical help. None of us knew what to do. Suddenly I thought of my World Peace Flame candle, lit it, and silently asked within myself for help. I intuitively started massaging reflex points on his feet, explaining to another traveller how to do the same on his hands. Soon he calmed down and within an hour went quietly back to sleep.

I was finding new faith in my inner power.

At the same time, my pain was getting lighter. The journey wasn't easy; I had to cope with blisters so bad I could hardly stand, shoulders aching from carrying my rucksack, and day after day of 44^0 heat. I regularly posted things from my rucksack home to lighten my load. At the same time, each day's progress seemed to lighten a little more of my 'immaterial load', my weight of grief and pain.

The turning point came at the top of the mountain. I took out the stone from Tycho's tree, gently held it to my heart and then placed it on the great cairn of stones left by centuries of other pilgrims before me. In this small action I was letting go of a lot of my grief, my pain... and also my son.

By the time I reached Santiago itself some days later I knew that most of my pain was healed.

After you lose something as precious as your son, a great space is left within you. On my healing journey, that space became filled with strengths I never knew I had. I discovered a new faith in myself and witnessed amazing transformations in others. I have so much more inner power and spiritual strength than I had before.

Yes, the price was very high. Nevertheless, I can feel that my son's light lives on, for his passing has brought so much healing and awakening to so many people.

It was just like him to want to help his friends.

Marlies v.d.S., The Netherlands

During Tycho's funeral, one of his teachers related the following incident:

'A week before he died, I met with Tycho to talk about his homework marks. I wanted to help him see that if he spent more time on his work he could easily get higher marks. He told me in response that marks of 60—70% were enough for him; he would rather spend the rest of his time with others, giving help and support to his friends, other students and even teachers.

'At the time I couldn't accept his answer, and tried to persuade him otherwise.

'Now I understand. Tycho taught me a big lesson that day.'

If you were going to die soon and had only one phone call you could make, who would you call and what would you say? And why are you waiting?

Stephen Levine

Rock Fall in a Coal Mine

Everything you do, everything you say, every moment of every hour gives you the power to transform your life completely.

In this story Siân Edwards, one of the Life Foundation's senior trainers, draws from her rich Welsh cultural heritage to show us how a single powerful experience can turn tragedy into a miracle and reshape people's lives across generations.

M any, many years ago, when my grandfather was a fourteen-year-old boy, he left school and worked in a coalmine in South Wales. This was not an exceptional occurrence—many children did this in order to support their families. In those days, each young lad worked with an older, very experienced 'partner', who would look after him and train him in his work. They would inevitably become the firmest of friends. Together, they worked in very dangerous circumstances, sometimes digging coal by hand in tunnels only three or four feet high, lying on their stomachs for many hours at a time. And so they often faced accidents together, some threatening their very lives.

The only source of light they had to work by in those early days was a coal miner's lamp with its single flickering flame; a lamp almost identical to the ones which house the World Peace Flame today. Not only did their lamp provide them with light to work by; the colour of its flame was their only warning of danger from explosive gasses or lack of oxygen in the tunnel. For this reason, every miner looked after his lamp as if it were his most valued and trusted friend.

One day, my grandfather and his older partner were working away at a very difficult seam in a tunnel with quite a low ceiling. They were in a notoriously unstable part of the mine and could only work as far as an old rock fall that had blocked the tunnel ahead of them.

As they neared this point, they suddenly heard the ominous rumbling of another rock fall. They looked back in horror as rocks tumbled down just behind them, trapping them in a tiny cavern bounded by the two falls.

Neither was hurt badly and so they scrambled to their knees and gazed at the flickering flame before them in their miner's lamp. And they prayed for their lives as they had never prayed before. They were in a very remote part of the mine, and rescue could take days. Imagine the feelings of my grandfather, a fourteen-year-old boy faced with his own mortality. Years later he often related to me how in those moments of extremity his only source of hope was their single, tiny flame.

Hours and hours passed with no sign of rescue, and their hearts continued to reach out to that small flame. Its light created shadows that moved as they moved and helped them feel less alone, as if other miners were in the shadows bringing them protection.

And then my grandfather became aware of a tiny, insistent voice tugging at his heart. It said, 'Start working on the old rock fall in front of you—it's much more stable than the one that fell behind you a few hours ago. Just move one rock at a time—you never know, you may find your way out of here.'

And so my grandfather started to move one rock at a time. It was a painstaking task, seemingly with no purpose. Yet he felt he had to do something. Later, he often described to me how that little voice within would not go away. He managed to clear away a small hole in the wall of rocks before him—just enough to hold the light up and peer through into what, he discovered, was another cavern beyond.

The sight he saw as he looked through this hole was to become one of the miracles of his (and my) life. For a few seconds, which seemed like an age to him, he saw two still, kneeling figures, dressed in clothes of an age gone by. One was an older man, the other a young boy about his own age. They were on their knees praying in front of an old miner's lamp.

Simultaneously, my grandfather heard the sound of rescuers working away at the rock fall behind him. As they broke through, a breeze entered his cavern and passed through the hole into the cavern beyond. And my grandfather saw both figures disintegrate into piles of dust before his very eyes...

He just knew in that moment that the prayers of that young boy and his partner had saved *his* life, another young boy caught in a mining accident so many years after they had lost their own lives.

He told his partner and all his other workmates what he had seen. They tried to put it down to the tricks of the mind and the shock of being in a life-threatening accident... However, the old miners did say that an accident had happened in that very tunnel some decades before and the bodies of two miners had never been recovered—one an older man and the other a young boy no older than my grandfather.

And so when I was a young girl, my grandfather used to teach me about the importance of having a living flame as a symbol of hope. I was never consciously aware of the seeds his story planted within me, yet over the years I found myself increasingly drawn to people who brought the light of hope to others. Neither my grandfather nor I knew then that I would later work with the Life Foundation and be part of bringing together the World Peace Flame. Yet in my heart I know that the prayers of my grandfather on that fateful day somehow had a hand in my own work today. Who knows how far-reaching our prayers can be? They can cross the oceans to the places where they are needed. They can also cross the ages into the future of our children.

So, when you gaze at the World Peace Flame, just know that your positive thoughts and prayers are making a difference. You will be helping someone in this world, no doubt, in ways you may never be able to conceive.

Siân Edwards, North Wales

Life can be so unstable at times that we all need a friend we can trust. For Siân's grandfather, light became that friend, giving him hope and guidance in the darkest moment of his life.

A single light shines brightly deep in the darkness of a mine, just as a single positive insight or act can begin to heal conflict or emotional turmoil. It only takes a moment to say 'I love you' and change somebody's life forever.

When you find yourself in crisis, it can make a huge difference if you decide to pull back for a moment and look at everything from a new perspective. Light a flame, pause for a few moments and reflect: 'What one thing can I do now that will add light to this situation?'

Sometimes, the tiniest act makes the biggest difference.

Rabbit

Maybe we like to be preoccupied with the great dramas of life, grappling with what is 'important'. Suppose, though, that the greatest moments of living happen even within the tiniest details. Then this charming story gives us a key to living that can fill our every moment with magic.

P eople have all sorts of animals for pets. A few years ago, I thought it would be nice to have a rabbit.

I went out to a local pet shop and bought a baby rabbit, along with a cage and everything else I'd need. However, after a few weeks the rabbit became unwell, as if she was paralysed. She lost her appetite and wasn't able to move around properly. She lost control of her legs, which began to move in all different directions, and soon she couldn't even hold her head up. When I took the rabbit to the vet, he told me she had injured her spine when jumping and that she wouldn't get better.

I returned home sadly. I couldn't face the thought of this poor rabbit never being able to walk or jump around again.

So I sat, stroking her gently, and put my Peace Flame by her. I asked the Flame to help her and give her strength. We must have sat together for an hour or so, and then slowly she began to lift up her head. I watched in wonder as she started to try to move her legs again—just feeble little movements at first, but co-ordinated, for the first time in days. Full of excitement, I tried giving her a piece of lettuce leaf, her favourite food. She ate it!

Two days after putting my Peace Flame by her, she jumped out of her cage and ran about the living room. As far as I was concerned it was a complete marvel; she had gone from death's door to jumping out of her cage in only two days. I knew the Peace Flame had helped her.

The vet could hardly believe what he saw when I took her in for a check up. He called it a miracle.

I smiled, because I knew what had happened.

My rabbit is still healthy, even today.

M.M., Scotland

Saint Francis of Assisi would never have bypassed a rabbit in distress! We often hear how great leaders through history—like Francis, Gandhi or Mother Teresa—never limited the size of their acts of caring. Their greatness came, in part, because they were willing to attend to the tiniest acts of kindness.

The World Peace Flame reminds us that its light shines equally on all.

A Call to Action

The ideas and policies of leaders of Parliament are often debated so widely that we can forget, a little, about their unique human strengths and aspirations. In this incident from an informal visit made by several European Parliamentarians to Auschwitz we discover how a profoundly transforming moment can come upon you even amidst the most painful surroundings.

Early in 2001 Andrew and I presented the World Peace Flame to one of the leaders of a European parliamentary party in his office in Brussels. With the Flame burning on his desk, he related a journey he and his family had made to the Auschwitz concentration camps in Poland, along with some other European Parliamentarians, a few years before.

The story touched us profoundly. We had also been to Auschwitz and could deeply empathise with his experiences. I don't think anyone could walk around those tiny cells, see the exhibits of human remains or visit the gas chambers of Birkenau without feeling the sheer weight of suffering that took place there. What can convey the feeling of standing on the place where more than a million people died?

'While we were there we organised an informal ceremony of light among ourselves,' he told us, 'in which we lit and left candles at the memorial to the dead in Auschwitz.'

When I asked him what light meant for him, his answer conveyed a depth of humanity I will always remember.

'My candle was lit by a survivor of the camps,' he replied.

'To me, it meant they were passing on—and I was receiving—the light of their experience.'

I have listened to the tape of our meeting many times since then, for his words carried a depth of human empathy that erased all boundaries and roles in an instant. He had stood there, one of Europe's senior politicians, surrounded by the weight of all that had happened in Auschwitz, holding a candle lit by someone who had experienced the awful reality of living there. In that moment, I feel sure, he had shared a moment of profound unity with this person and taken the light of their experiences into himself.

Throughout the day, he and his family walked around the camp with an elderly woman who had survived the camps but had lost all her family there. She was well into her seventies, yet had not been back since. 'Just to watch her for the day,' he said, 'was almost to experience the whole depth of her emotions.'

Later in the day, she carefully made her way over the rubble to reach the centre of one of the gas chambers, which now looks like a ruined building site. After all the events of their visit, the sight affected him deeply. He watched her small, frail figure. 'She took from her pocket a small candle and one flower. And she lit the candle.

'I still feel it emotionally,' he continued. 'There were so many things you could take, but finally this moment was so private and so moving that she deserved to be alone.

'I had to turn away.'

I felt him in the scene, watching that frail, elderly woman as she lit her lonely candle in the middle of all that desolation. Who could know what she was remembering in that moment with her candle and her flower? What purpose could it serve?

'For me it was a symbol,' he concluded, 'that this was more than just a very emotional moment. It was a call to duty, a call to be the one who puts a light in the window or rings a bell to summon your community to action.'

Savitri MacCuish

Have you ever felt a call to action?

These calls can be gateways to some of the most fulfilling and rewarding experiences in our lives. Perhaps you once saw someone die innocently in a war or a famine and thought, 'Right, that's it. I'm going to do something now!' Or maybe you were once touched by the plight of people suffering from an illness or a disability and moved heaven and earth to help them.

An unparalleled joy comes from completing such a call to action, or from seeing real gratitude in the eyes of someone you have helped.

WITH CHILDREN AND THE FAMILY

" *You are the light in the Lord;
walk as children of light.* "

St Paul

How to Win at Football

Look closely at the thinking of a child. Children live in a world without borders—a world that has a 360 degree perspective on everything—and they can think in ways that embrace concepts adults might never dream of. As a result, the problems of life are not hard for a child to solve. How's your football going?

The World Peace Flame

The World Peace Flame is for strength and hope.

I usually light candles just because it is cosy.

First we thought Grandpa was going to die and then we lit three candles.

Now I think Grandpa will be eighty, he is seventy now.

The fireplace is a big flame.

It's nice and warm and gives you strength.

If we light the fireplace on Friday night,

I win playing football on Saturday.

And when we had not lit it I lost.

Candles give you strength and hope.

Jan, age 11

Hedgehogs

Hey, hedgehogs

You all know we get the Peace Flame today.

I think it is exciting...

And we, the hedgehogs from the hedgehog classroom, get the Peace Flame

As the first in the Netherlands...

It was nice when the Peace Flame arrived with us.

It was very quiet when the beeswax candle was lit.

Everyone had to think of someone you wanted to send it to.

Nearly everyone thought of Tim, who was ill at that time and guess what happened.

Exactly.

He was in school again the next morning.

Sharon, age 10

The Peace Flame

The Peace Flame means for me rest and peace.

Light a candle and keep watching it.

Then I get a warm feeling inside.

And if I think of something pitiful,

The tears come into my eyes.

The Peace Flame started in Wales.

We are the first in the Netherlands that get the Peace Flame.

I found it a very special moment.

Philippa, age 11

Do you still remember how to win at football?

Mahatma Gandhi always made time to be around children so he would remember to think with their innocence and creativity. Kids dance, paint, write, laugh and make fun as though there is no tomorrow. They have a 'unified' view of the world because their hearts and minds are one collective whole.

If you are getting a little heavy in your thinking, try taking a ten-minute walk and remembering how you saw nature when you were young. Weren't those dust motes in a sunbeam fairies…? or light-ships to another world? Weren't those piles of leaves there just for you to scuffle through? Weren't butterflies made just to make you laugh?

With a child's perspective your problems feel smaller and your solutions carry further.

Peace Begins at Home

I have been lighting my World Peace Flame candle every day for a year or two now, and have just begun to discover a very handy use for the Flame.

If my family becomes a bit 'noisy'—which can be quite draining after a long day (especially at teatime when the children get tired)—I've learned that if I light my Peace Flame then the feeling in the house seems to be a lot smoother and more 'manageable'.

It is such a comforting thought to know that I can use my Peace Flame for the smaller things in my life as well as for the much larger arena of world peace.

But then, doesn't peace begin at home?

V.M., Scotland

Are there any 'little things' in your life that you wish were more peaceful? Light a flame and give it a try!

This experience will be most effective for you when it rests upon a daily practice of connecting with the power of light. You might like to try the ideas and meditations presented in Part 3.

Jimmy and the Peace Flame

Have you ever been presented with a good idea that you really would rather not be bothered with? Sometimes we need a little help before we'll take up the opportunities we are offered.

Eight-year-old Jimmy rushed home from school, banged open the door and began to shout without a pause, 'Mum! Mum! My best friend Mark has got a special candle it's called the World Peace Flame and he has to light it every day so there will be no more fighting and can I have one too?'

Mary looked at her little son, smiling at his exuberance. 'Calm down,' she said. 'Take off your coat and we'll have a drink. Let's sit down together and you can tell me all about it more slowly.' Jimmy often came home from school excited about his day, and his mother had learnt long ago that if they sat quietly for a time he would settle down enough for his stories to make more sense.

However, Jimmy wasn't so easily stopped. He continued to talk non-stop about the World Peace Flame and how much he wanted one. The following morning as he left for school he said, 'Mum, when you go shopping please buy me a Peace Flame.'

Mary shook her head, 'I don't know what to do, Jimmy,' she said, secretly hoping he would forget all about it. 'I don't know any shops that sell World Peace Flames.'

However, every day for the next three days he talked about it and pleaded with her to buy him one.

That very Saturday, Mary walked into an exhibition in Perth. There, for free, was a big display of World Peace Flame candles! She couldn't believe her eyes.

Of course, she made a bee-line for the exhibition and was soon eagerly asking questions and listening to the story of the Flame's journey. The vision at last came alive for her. That evening, she gave Jimmy his special present.

Each day now they sit and pray together for peace. 'Its given me a special time to be with my son,' says Mary, 'and started me doing something for the world I might never otherwise have done.'

E.R., Scotland

How many good ideas have you never followed up for one reason or other? Try writing some of them down and then look for ways to follow them through. You may find that they can lead you to the same joy that Mary found in her relationship with Jimmy.

When I Learnt to Love My Mother

*There is no greater miracle than the return of love. You will see in this beautiful experience how such a return of love was not won easily. It required patient nurturing, day after day, over many months. Yet what price can we put on such a gift? We are sure you would agree that **any** effort would have been worth the outcome you will read here.*

The first time I ever remember feeling love for my mother was when I was twelve.

Growing up as the eldest of seven children in a small village in The Netherlands, I can honestly say I can hardly recall a single positive encounter between my mother and any of us children. It was as if some sort of cage surrounded her that made it impossible for her to show any affection towards us.

When I was twelve my mother became ill. She started to faint a lot and began to need many hours of rest. Once, she fainted near the top of the stairs and I remember holding her in my arms saying, 'Mum, Mum, this is not right.'

She was diagnosed with cancer. In those days there was nothing available like chemotherapy or radiation treatment. Bravely, she said, 'I'll go to Lourdes, and pray to Mother Mary. When I come back I will be cured because I cannot leave my boys alone to fend for themselves.'

In my lonely twelve-year-old world I knew nothing about her own personal friendships, joys or struggles. Yet she must have been well-respected in our community because the doctor's wife offered to pay for her trip and made sure she had support along the way. And, although I never saw it, she must have loved us with an unbelievable strength, because when she came back from Lourdes the cancer had gone, so strong was her faith in God.

After that, life went on as before. She was always there to provide for us, but her lack of affection left me with a coldness in my heart that hardened during my teens and stayed with me across the years. Perhaps unconsciously perceiving this, she became increasingly demanding and insistent that I visit her regularly. I'm fairly soft-hearted so I found it hard to refuse her, yet as a result my inner coldness deepened. I began to find visiting her distasteful and to feel repulsed if ever I had to embrace her.

Nearly forty years later I was given a World Peace Flame candle and as I looked into its light for the first time a vivid memory came flooding back. Suddenly, there I was again at the top of the stairs all those years before, holding my mother, my heart breaking with my desperation to feel her warmth and her breath forever. Then I remembered the way she came back from Lourdes, so full of faith, and I remembered how her cancer had gone away.

In that moment, all the intervening years of hardness seemed to melt away and I found myself yearning to feel again that love for my mother. I knew that somehow this small candle could help me. The idea of all the love of the people who light this flame really captivated me. I knew, without knowing how I knew, that its light could help me learn to love my mother again.

From that moment on, as I began to use the World Peace Flame, something began to heal within me, little by little. Every day I would take a few moments to sit with the candle and pray—I don't know to whom—for my love to come back. I would visualise my mother surrounded by the same light as I saw in the candle, and I would see myself close beside her.

Gradually, the light of the World Peace Flame in my house became a solid, stabilising symbol of the existence of love. I became more and more certain I would someday regain the ability to feel love again myself.

Then, not long ago, a moment came when I realised I was ready. Right down to the very core of my heart, I was ready to forgive her and let my love flow to her. I felt a fullness and strength that I hadn't experienced before. For the first time in decades I actually wanted to go and visit my mother.

I still don't really recall the precise details of what each of us said to the other on that special visit. All I know is that at one moment I just blurted out, 'Mum, I forgive you for everything!' and rushed over and held her in my arms.

She stiffened just for a moment and then her whole body relaxed into my arms, just as if the hard cage surrounding her heart was being dismantled. For the first time in my adult life I could feel love for her flowing from the bottom of my heart, and in response I could feel her own love flowing back to me just as strongly through her own embrace. It was the first time in my life that I ever recall feeling a reciprocal love with my mother. The wall between us had been broken away forever.

A healing occurred that day that has not left us. Now I know that if one of us were to die it would be okay. The healing we each yearned for has happened and our relationship has become complete.

My mother's presence in my life, I feel, has been saved by a second miracle. The first time the Madonna in Lourdes brought her back to me. This time it was the World Peace Flame.

L.S., The Netherlands

What a relief to discover that love can return even to the most closed heart. In fact, a love regained can be the sweetest of all loves. This son's experience shows us three great principles for healing a hardened heart.

- ❖ *It is important to **know** that the healing you yearn for is possible.*
- ❖ *It is necessary to **want** this healing—even if you don't feel anything positive to start with!*
- ❖ *It is important to **ask** for help.*

The World Peace Flame gives you access to that place within yourself where you can co-create your own destiny. Any healing you ask for within this place will be granted if you give it all your faith, confidence and trust.

'Make Sure No-one Ever Stops You'

Have you ever experienced how a few well-placed words from a friend can be all that's needed to open whole new vistas in your life?

My family and I were present at the Life Foundation Conference in 1999 when the World Peace Flame was created.

At the moment we were about to walk into the Main Hall for the ceremony to unite the Flames, my ten-year-old son Bram went very quiet. He was supposed to leave us and continue onwards with his sister to the children's programme.

Instead he stood still and said, 'Mum, you don't really think I'm going to miss this do you?'

It put us in a dilemma. Children didn't usually go into the sessions in the Main Hall.

At that moment John Jones, one of the Life Foundation's senior trainers, walked past. I told him of Bram's request. John smiled at Bram encouragingly and said, 'If you find something you really want to go for, make sure no-one ever stops you.'

Bram looked very satisfied at his words, boldly walked through the door into the Hall and headed straight for the seats at the front.

I watched Bram many times during the ceremony, which obviously made a profound impact upon him. Since that moment he has made a deep 'friendship'—it is the only word I can think of—with the World Peace Flame, and regularly sits

in silence with it in his room before he goes to sleep.
This is how Bram described his experiences.

When I was ten years old I was there when the World Peace
Flame came into being. It was really amazing. I did not exactly
understand why, but I felt it.

When I came back from my holiday I did a talk on the World
Peace Flame in school because I wanted everyone to know
about it.

I always feel very closely connected with the World Peace
Flame because first of all it always burns in our house and
because my mum works with the Life people.

My own experience is that I can always fall back on it when
I've got difficulties or when something is happening.

For instance, my friend has been very ill for a few years now.
A few months ago, when I heard that he was probably going
to die, I started to look at the World Peace Flame for one
minute nearly every day and asked for help for this friend.
Shortly afterwards I heard that they found something that
would help cure his illness.

I am convinced that light has an enormous power inside.

A.S., The Netherlands

*Imagine if neither Bram nor John had spoken on that morning.
One young man's life might have missed out on countless special
moments. And what about his friend?*

Healing Arguments in Our Relationship

When we have an argument in our relationship, the first thing we do is light the Peace Flame.

It gives us the feeling that there is a witness to our dilemma, a benevolent presence that will listen impartially to us both.

Just having this comforting thought in the back of our minds enables us to come out of our own corners and become more willing to look at each other's side of things. We find the Flame helps us remember that there is a loving presence within the universe that will always come to our aid. With this, it is easier to come through all the emotions and open our hearts to what each other is saying.

Isn't that the solution to all problems, having the openness to look at other perspectives? It helps us get out of the 'either-or' dilemma, and discover an 'and-and' solution.

Truth has got more than one face, and our relationship works best when we remember this!

C.S. and A.E., England

When you feel disturbed by conflict or argument, try lighting a Flame and gazing into its golden light. After a while, send some positive thoughts to the person you are in conflict with. Ask for help in solving the situation. Watch for flashes of intuition that suggest a new way forward—and follow them.

The Girl with Special Needs

*Have you ever come across a young person so hurt that they have
closed off from life? You would do anything to help them find their
way back. The World Peace Flame is a tool that can help you
sharpen your sensitivity in these situations. It helps you say the
right thing at the right time and in the right place. Have a look at
how this special needs educator helped a young friend completely
turn her life around as a result of this kind of sensitivity.*

For many years I have worked for my Local Education
Authority as a teacher of children with special needs. The
job involves working one-to-one with my pupils, usually in
their homes. There are many reasons why children come to
me—some of them have been expelled from school for behav-
ioural reasons, some have chronic illnesses, others are 'school
refusers'. All have severe problems which, if unresolved, will
limit their potential for the rest of their lives.

When I met Jane she was fourteen years old and had been
more or less housebound for years. She had been bullied at
school and, being a very sensitive child, had withdrawn into
her own world, watching television for hours on end and playing computer games. She left the house infrequently, and then
only in the company of her parents. Jane was academically far
behind her age group, partly because she was on medication
for a chronic illness, and partly because she lacked self-confi-
dence and was therefore afraid to try anything at which she
might fail.

We had to begin almost from scratch, learning how to write the letters of the alphabet correctly, tackling very basic arithmetic, looking at money—and even how to tell the time. Right from the start I took a World Peace Flame candle with me to our lessons. Jane would light it before we began to work, and it would burn quietly during our time together. Sometimes, during our breaks, we would just gaze at it. I felt very sure that its peaceful and calming energies were helping Jane to relax, to lose her fear and to concentrate more deeply.

Slowly but steadily her work improved. Soon her reading became much more fluent and expressive. Her writing, which had been almost illegible, was now neat and she was even able to use punctuation and paragraphing reasonably accurately. Her maths came on in leaps and bounds, and she was especially pleased with herself when she mastered basic skills like using money correctly and telling the time.

However, it was still almost impossible to get Jane out of the house. Even on a sunny summer's day she would refuse to sit outside—and there was no way she would socialise. Jane had no friends. I persisted in my contact with the Flame while we worked, often silently asking it to help her, or gazing at it and mentally bathing her in its light. Nevertheless, Jane didn't seem able to make the final transformation. She was isolated, and her life was very lonely.

However, I have found that the World Peace Flame is a creator of miracles. One day, I 'happened' to meet a very old friend of mine in our local supermarket. He and I stood there by the bread counter and started catching up on everything that had been happening in our lives since last we met. Eventually, the conversation got round to work and I told him about my job, mentioning Jane as I did so. His face lit up as I spoke. 'The Lord is kind!' he exclaimed with a huge grin. He had just begun work in a centre for people with special needs, he said, and they were looking for a young person to help in their café. Jane fitted the bill perfectly.

A couple of days later I asked Jane if she would like to come with me to look at the café. To my surprise, she agreed. Set in the woodlands in the middle of a beautiful park, it was a haven of peace and tranquillity. The staff were warm, friendly and welcoming—and soon Jane was feeling so at home that she was even smiling at the other young people who worked there. I asked if she would like to come and help for one or two days a week, and she readily agreed. She was so keen that she wanted to start straight away! I could hardly believe it—the impossible was actually happening.

After that, Jane never looked back. Soon, she increased her time there to four days per week and was even able to travel there alone. She and I continued to spend some time each week on school work, and she was able to pass a couple of exams before she reached school-leaving age.

Jane is still at the café. She works there full-time, and has become a skilled and efficient assistant, much appreciated by her colleagues. When I visited her this Christmas she proudly showed me the shelf-full of cards she had received from all her friends. Her life has opened up and she is now becoming an independent and happy young woman.

When I think of her transformation—which took place in less than two years—and remember that 'chance' meeting with my old friend, I know that miracles can happen. Nothing is impossible when you are working with the World Peace Flame.

Rob.M, Canada

One day, like Rob, we may be the one who is given both the opportunity and the circumstances to rekindle the light within a child's

life. He used three key principles we can learn from.

- ❖ *He made a **constant effort** in his connection with the World Peace Flame. Day by day he refined his ability to sense what Jane needed.*
- ❖ *He was **continuously interested** in finding a solution for her.*
- ❖ *He was **certain** that eventually a solution would come. Such trust has a way of literally pulling the right result towards you.*

The light of glory shines in
the middle of the night.
Who sees it?
A heart that has eyes and waits.

Angelus Silesius
17th Century

Feeling Warm Inside Again

I was six years old when the Flame came into being.

When I saw the Flame for the very first time I got very happy inside. It was as if I saw angels dancing within the Flame.

That night, I dreamt that the Light of the Flame would spread around the entire earth.

When something bad happens, I sit still with the Flame.

Also when I am angry.

My rabbit just died. I found that really horrible because I loved my rabbit very much. Even Mum and Dad could not comfort me. When I went to sit with the Flame I got warm inside again.

I always have only one wish and that is Peace.

Love from Sofie.

Sofie, age 8, The Netherlands

AT WORK
OR STUDY

" Let nothing pass for every hand must
find some work to do;
Lose not a chance to waken love—be
firm, and just, and true:
So shall a light that cannot fade,
beam on thee from on high.
And angel voices say to thee—
these things shall never die. "

Charles Dickens

Within the Doctor's Surgery

When you seek a healing balm, look first within to your own inner strength. In this story, we see how the presence of the World Peace Flame can help remind people to help themselves in one of the places we most commonly give our power away—the doctor's surgery.

All doctors, just about anywhere in the world, are familiar with the experience of having so many patients in their waiting room that they have virtually no time to build quality, healing relationships with the people who come to see them.

For my husband, Robert, a G.P. for thirty years, the World Peace Flame turned everything around.

Like many doctors, Robert has a marvellous combination of deep sensitivity and immense pragmatism within his character. I often think of him as my 'great experimenter'. So a few years ago when he first heard of how the World Peace Flame helps to remind people of their inner strength, he decided to give it a try. He began to keep World Peace Flame candles alight continuously in both his surgery and his waiting room, and started giving small candles lit from the Flame to his patients when it was appropriate.

The results were so dramatic they startled even him.

Only days after he introduced the Flame, the atmosphere in his practice began to change. In the waiting room, the practice manager was struck by how the patients became milder and complained less.

In Robert's consulting room the difference was remarkable. It is quite common for patients to come into the doctor's surgery full of complaints, launching into a volley of symptoms with the unspoken expectation that the doctor will take complete responsibility for their health. Now he found patients taking a different attitude. Instead of expecting to be 'fixed', they would approach him with an attitude of 'would you be able to help me with…?' as if wanting to take responsibility for healing themselves. The extraordinary thing, Robert confided, was that this change seemed to occur across the board, even in those patients who didn't notice the candle burning quietly in his room.

We were staggered by the effectiveness of his experiment. Within a short while, we even began to hear people commenting regularly on how healing and peaceful they found the atmosphere of the clinic, wondering why it no longer seemed so busy and intense. We weren't at all sure they would believe our answer!

Perhaps the greatest changes occurred with patients to whom Robert personally handed a World Peace Flame candle. People in the final stage of a terminal illness would find strength and solace in its light. Patients suffering from stress would find a degree of calm. And most remarkable of all were people who came in with emotional problems.

For instance, when people came in suffering from depression Robert would offer them anti-depressant medication, and also advise them on how to build a healing relationship with themselves. When he wrote out the prescription he would add a line or two for the Flame: 'Look at it for a few moments each day for two to three weeks with the feelings that you appreciate and honour yourself.' He would always add, 'Then let me know how you are getting on.'

Within days he would get calls from people saying their lives were changing; they were beginning to climb out of the hole they had been in. They rarely needed repeat prescriptions.

You can imagine how much the patients loved my husband's warmth and care. However, he could never feel satisfied that he was able to help them with their deeper needs given the intense time constraints of a busy medical practice. He became increasingly tired and eager for a change.

We tried having a locum for a year to cover one day per week, so he could explore other therapies based more on a whole-person approach. We tried to find a suitable successor but no matter how hard we looked we couldn't find the right person. Finally, on the week the locum was due to finish his year, we resolved to leave the practice whether or not we found an adequate replacement.

That same week, a friend passed the name of a visiting doctor to me. Apparently he was thinking of moving to our area.

We rang him immediately, explaining our situation, and invited him over to meet us. As is our habit, we had the World Peace Flame burning near our dining table, and its warm, healing glow soon helped to create a marvellous rapport between us. By the end of the night he was so enthusiastic that he wanted to visit the practice with his wife.

A few days later we met at the practice. It was obvious that the doctor was deeply moved by his conversations with the staff and some of the patients, as well as by its healing atmosphere.

Suddenly, he turned to us and we could feel his words coming so spontaneously from his heart that he was as surprised as us to be hearing them. 'I want to start immediately,' he said. 'I don't know why, but the atmosphere and everything here suits me so completely that I don't want to waste any more time.'

We were amazed. He was amazed. But we all knew this was the right thing to be happening. Normally it takes four months to transfer a practice over to another doctor. In our case everything was completed in just over three weeks.

Now, we run a new kind of therapy centre. Patients come in

for hour-long consultations, and Robert gives them acupuncture, yoga practices, counselling sessions... and, as often as not, a World Peace Flame.

After all, it had helped him in his healing quest.

J.M and R.M., Canada

If you are engaged in any kind of business involving people, try bringing the World Peace Flame onto the scene. Notice how new ideas start to unfold to create opportunities for everyone to fulfil their most cherished dreams.

A Remarkable Exam Result

A wise person once said, 'The best form of hope is born from good preparation.' Imagine if you had a wise teacher standing by your side to help you in your studies—and then imagine that this teacher joined you invisibly in your exams, to whisper answers just when you needed them. Here is one student's experience.

During a seminar for young people in my homeland of The Netherlands, Mansukh Patel described how he used to study and work with a flame when he was at university. He gave us some small pointers that had made a big difference to his study results at the time.

One of the things he had found most helpful was to burn a light on his desk while he was studying. So, when my next university exams came round I decided I would try it out. Every time I delved into my books, I would keep a lighted candle by my desk[1].

The World Peace Flame has been burning day and night for a few years in my parents' house, so I decided to light my candle from this flame. Whenever I lacked concentration, I would pause and look at the light and imagine it represented a wise friend studying alongside me, gaining the knowledge I was trying to absorb. I soon discovered that my concentration level improved enormously with the flame present in my room. For

---

[1] Safety note: Please remember to only use a lighted flame in an enclosed lamp on a flame-proof tray. Keep it away from papers at all times and never leave a burning flame unattended.

days on end, from early morning till late at night, I would lock myself into my room and study in this way. I even settled into a new rhythm: rise early, do some yoga with one of my parents, have a light breakfast and then back into the books with the light burning by my desk.

During an exam I would visualise this light, asking her if she would help me. When I arrived at a question and did not know what to do I would think of the flame at which I had gazed so many times during my studying. Most of the times I found that the right answer would come.

My exam results were very positive. I advise everyone to use light as a study companion!

C.d.R., The Netherlands

Light can help us access powers of mind far beyond our norm. It stimulates the pineal and pituitary glands, master controllers of the whole endocrine system. When you call on the World Peace Flame to help you in this way, as this young woman did, you open up the part of your mind that is capable of rapid learning and complete retention.

Light reveals and unveils the hidden knowledge within us.

John O'Donohue

End to Bullying

Bullying at work can lead to the most devastating fear. Sometimes, the key step in solving the problem is healing the fear itself. Read how one person ended up in the right place at the right time to help her sister overcome her fear so she could reach out for the help that was already available.

I first realised the power of the World Peace Flame as a won-derful tool in my life about three years ago.

Shortly after the World Peace Flame was born, I heard about it in an evening Dru Yoga class I was attending near Glasgow, Scotland. Our teacher gave each of us a small candle lit from the Flame as well as a leaflet telling us all about it.

I remember feeling quite impressed by the story but as I left the class I put the little candle in my pocket—as you do—and sort of forgot about it for a while. One morning I was clearing out my pockets and I lifted out the candle and leaflet, thinking that I might as well light it. I placed it in a prime position on my dressing table.

I remember gazing at this little flame and noticing how it seemed so 'still' while at the same time being so powerfully bright.

After a minute or so I put the candle out and as I did so, I was suddenly struck by the thought of all the other people around the world who have this same flame burning in their homes. Somehow I knew this was a most precious little object.

I then set off on my daily routine, taking my young children to school and nursery and then heading onwards for a morning swim at the local swimming pool. However, on my journey there I absently took a wrong turning and found myself en route to my sister's house. Before I knew it I was parked outside her house, wondering what on earth had made me come this way. Shrugging my shoulders, I popped in for a visit.

I knocked on her back door and finding no reply pushed it open and walked into her kitchen. My sister was sitting by herself in tears. I comforted her and spoke to her for a long time before she was willing to say why she was so upset.

Eventually she told me that she was being bullied at work. She was full of fear. I sat by her and held her, and began to assure her that everything would be okay. The bullying had been going on for some time, and I told her that all she needed to do was talk to her superiors who would be able to deal properly with the matter.

After a couple of hours and some continuous persuasion, my sister finally picked up the phone and spoke to her manager, who immediately arranged to see her that same afternoon.

Forty-eight hours later there was a further meeting which included the person who had instigated the bullying and from there they were able to completely resolve the situation.

I was amazed when I heard the news. In my heart of hearts I knew there was no coincidence between lighting my World Peace Flame on that morning and being guided to my sister's side in her time of need. Because of our conversation that morning, she was able to realise her own potential and strength and do the right things to get everything resolved. In fact, she had already been surrounded by all the help she needed. She just needed the courage to ask for it.

As a result of this I introduced my sister to the World Peace Flame, which now burns in her own home.

Ever since that morning I have lit my Flame daily for the whole world and try to send out its light to whoever might be in need. Why? Because I discovered on that memorable day that even though it looks tiny, the power of this Flame can be felt wherever it is sent.

K.S., Scotland

Every difficulty we ever encounter, no matter how challenging, will always carry within it the seeds of its own resolution. Always. The art of living lies in knowing how to find these seeds, and then nurturing them carefully until they bloom.

The light of a flame eases away any darkness between you and these seeds, so you can more easily find the solutions that lie so plentifully around you.

Ice Creams on Fire

Every moment can make somebody's life magical. Here's one way,
experienced by a colleague of ours. What are yours?

On the day after completing one of our seminars, I met
with my colleagues, Deb, Ron, Jeannie and Ned at an
ice-cream shop to celebrate and relax.

Ned had been presenting the World Peace Flame to a group
nearby and so had it with him, quietly burning within its
miner's lantern. Our young waiter was fascinated by the Flame
and wanted to know all about it. We talked to him for a while
and then he went off to fetch our order.

After a few minutes the Flame dimmed and went very blue,
running out of fuel. One of us said, 'Never mind, the light is
firmly established in our hearts.'

No sooner was this said than the young waiter returned
with a huge smile on his face carrying our ice-creams, each
with *live flames* on top, flambé style.

We were in stitches! You can never put out the light.

P.M., England

When was the last time you sat down and had a really hearty belly
laugh? If it was more than an hour or two ago, then put this book
down immediately and go and give someone an ice cream on fire!

The Film that Stopped the Rain

This Dutch film-maker made a decision near the climax of a long and distinguished career to stop making films unless they created a positive and inspirational response in his viewers. His decision has had such a far-reaching effect that it has helped instigate a whole new genre of films on Dutch television. Here, he mentions several principles that help keep his work flowing with the natural stream of life.

Movie production is determined to a large extent by how many days are available for filming. When you ask a film-maker on the last day of filming if he or she has filmed everything in their script they will invariably say 'no.' There are always unforeseen setbacks: a camera running out of batteries, people arriving late on the set or the inevitable waiting for the right lighting conditions.

During the filming of 'The Heart of the Matter—A Matter of Heart' one February in North Wales, our biggest source of setbacks was the weather. Hoping for good weather in a Welsh winter is a sign of deep faith and my wife Louise, producer of the film, was in an almost constant state of controlled panic trying to juggle the required filming into the few moments of good weather we had available. The rain seemed continuously horizontal and the wind regularly rose to Storm Force Ten.

The weather was as bad as it had ever been on the day that Mansukh, Savitri and friends were due to hand the World Peace Flame over to Andrew and three others who would begin walking it to The Hague in the Netherlands.

This unique moment was vital to the film and could not be missed. Could the transfer happen the following day? That was not an option. We would somehow have to make do. Our cameraman, Devadatta Visser, packed his camera in water-proof plastic. We bought umbrellas, silently sent out a plea for the right conditions and drove off towards the mountain pass where the handover was due to take place.

As we drove, the windscreen wipers hardly made any impression on the curtain of water pouring down on us. We pictured Mansukh and Savitri walking up the other side of the valley with the World Peace Flame torch. How could anyone keep a torch burning in this weather? I was well aware that this film scene, literally and figuratively speaking, could become a total washout. Even though we all thought the same, no-one said a word. From experience we have learned that you can invite disappointment by giving in to cynicism.

Once we arrived at the place where the transfer was to take place we looked for the best spot to set up the camera and then gazed into the distance. Visibility was hopeless. Somewhere Savitri, Mansukh and their friends were trudging through the pouring rain in the cold wind and we had to film them. The wind tugged at the camera on its tripod as Devadatta pointed his long-focus lens onto a place where he thought their path might be. His grumbling didn't augur well for us. 'Let's face it,' I thought to myself, 'there is not much more to be seen than a flood of water moving horizontally through the air.' With a supreme effort, I decided to remain optimistic, reminding myself that you never know…

At that moment a robin flew by and positioned himself in the tree right behind us. Jauntily he looked down and started his flute concerto. Then I heard Devadatta say, 'There they are…' and a little later, 'Believe it or not, their torch is burn-ing…' When they came closer we could see it burning with our own eyes. The little bird behind us jumped from branch to branch. Suddenly, there was a lull in the weather.

What happened? How could the wind have subsided so suddenly? Why did the rain nearly stop all of a sudden? For the ten minutes or so that it took Mansukh, Savitri and Andrew to meet each other the wind calmed down and the rain softened to a fine mist. We even had time to find a second camera position so we could film their short dialogue as the torch was passed over. Everything worked without a hitch. Even the drops of water that landed on the lens arranged themselves perfectly to make the shots more artistic.

We did what we had to do. At the moment the World Peace Flame was transferred, birds were singing in the trees as though it were a beautiful spring day[1].

And then, as soon as we had filmed the Peace Flame disappearing into the distance on its long journey towards The Netherlands, we hurriedly began to pack our equipment. The wind was beginning to resume its strength and soon the rain once again poured from left to right. The birds had gone.

I looked at Mansukh and Savitri. They smiled, shrugged their shoulders almost unnoticeably and said, 'You really should get back. You are soaking wet…'

It was time to get on with the rest of the filming.

P. Engelen, The Netherlands

How can you tell whether or not your work is moving in a direction that is 'right'? One of the most useful points to observe is what is being referred to now as 'support-in-nature'. If the circum-

---

[1] The scene described here can be seen in the beginning of the film *The Heart of the Matter - A Matter of Heart,* available from Life Foundation Publications.

stances of the natural world seem to clear a path for your actions, you can be pretty sure your activity is flowing in harmony with life.

Mansukh's father used to say that the universe has only three responses to your thoughts: 'Yes! Yes! and Yes!'

We have found that the real challenge in life is getting all your thoughts—conscious and unconscious—to say the same thing! You can use a brief time of silence to disengage from the chattering mind. Breathe in courage, energy, love and certainty and breathe out through the mouth, letting go of anxiety or agitation.

> *As fire lights the wood it consumes, so the soul illuminates the body with consciousness.*
>
> Srimad Bhagavatam

The Tax Inspection

When you live in a world of taking, it is quite natural that life is likely to take from you. Conversely, here is a superb example of how giving to life always helps you. Even during a visit of the tax inspector.

I n my region, every citizen who is self-employed has to undergo a full scrutiny by the tax office every four years. Last year it was our turn.

Our accountant informed us of the impending visit and prepared us for the fact that the tax inspector who would be conducting our interview was notorious in his field. He had asked for a full two-day meeting to scrutinise every detail of our home counselling business within the past four years.

Our first impressions of the tax inspector as he entered our house immediately confirmed his reputation. He wore a long, black, leather coat, had a robust stature and a fixed and stern face. Years of working in hostile environments had obviously trained him to be a very suspicious man.

In response, we had decided to try a different approach.

For a number of years we have kept candles lit from the World Peace Flame in a central position in our main room. People have often remarked to us how much the atmosphere in our house has changed. They say it is calmer and more peaceful. Conversations happen differently in the presence of the Flame. Disagreements are less likely, we find, and when they occur, the people involved are more interested in looking for a solution than in blaming each other.

Usually people are not very happy when they receive a visit from a tax inspector, who is paid to discover discrepancies within the company's finances and hence make more money for the government. We wanted to try to make our tax inspection experience a warm and memorable occasion.

Much to the surprise of the inspector, we gave him a warm welcome and immediately offered coffee and biscuits to him, his assistant and our accountant, who had joined us for the meeting. The inspector lost no time getting into our administration and began to look for the usual tell-tale signs of miscalculations or dishonesty. We answered his questions politely, enthusiastically adding a little about our work whenever we could. I told him about the World Peace Flame and the inspiration it was giving us to follow a simpler lifestyle.

My husband talked about how we got more pleasure out of our voluntary work with charities than in spending our money. Although our business is very successful and makes a considerable amount of money by normal standards, it was clear to him that we were giving away a substantial amount and were not using more than we needed for a comfortable lifestyle. 'I can see you are not investing it in expensive furnishings or activities,' he remarked with growing warmth. 'But you know, if you give away more than 13.5% you can't count the rest as a tax deduction!'

We responded truthfully that we had never asked for such a deduction, and began to tell him about some of the other charities we support. He pounced on a recent trip to South America which we had put down as a business expense—we had been gathering new therapeutic ideas while we were there—and we told him about some of our work supporting poorer villages in the area. Each time he thought he might have found a false or misleading statement, it turned out to be another opportunity for us to talk about how much we enjoyed our humanitarian activities.

As the morning wore on we could feel his attitude changing. Gradually, glimmers of a smile began to appear, and he began to ask for our presence by his side while he worked. 'It helps me to get to the bottom of my queries faster,' he said, but we began to suspect he had an ulterior motive. He was simply enjoying being with people who were kind to him. It wasn't long before we were having a constant dialogue about our lives and the business. He even began to show us places where we could save tax!

Finally, he came to the point in the business where it was clear that we were about to take a decision to change our direction and branch out into other therapeutic ventures. 'But this is not going to help your financial situation at all,' he protested, his suspicions never quite disappearing.

'Yes, we are well aware of that,' I responded. The two of us had thought about this difficult decision long and hard. 'We feel we're ready for a change, and want to move onwards now to new therapies that will help us to bring a greater benefit to people.'

'You're taking a huge financial risk,' he commented.

'We know, but we've learnt to trust,' was my response. 'If you help the world,' I said, 'you always find help comes to you when you need it.'

He was silent at that, but we could both see the comment had landed deeply.

After lunch the inspector spent another half-hour going through our papers. Then, to our surprise, he abruptly closed all the books and stood up. He had seen enough, he declared, and wouldn't need to come back the next day after all.

As the tax officer and his assistant got ready to depart, we asked them to pause for a moment. We took them over to the World Peace Flame and gave them each candles lit from it— which they accepted as precious gifts.

Two days later our accountant phoned us, still astonished by the experience. 'I have been in countless meetings with my clients and that man,' he said, 'and I have never seen anything like it. Normally he takes two days and makes people pay huge tax bills. This time, he took five hours and ended up helping you save money!'

These were wonderful outcomes, no doubt, but to us there was an even greater one. As he left our house, we had seen a look of warmth and a renewed interest in living in our tax inspector's eyes.

M.R., Belgium

Light, which shines on everyone unconditionally, teaches us the principles of giving. Once we enter a world of giving, we find it is a two-way principle: as you give, so you receive.

Since the way we interact with others creates their response, it is worth preparing yourself for a few moments before an important meeting—with a World Peace Flame if you have one. Visualise the outcome you want from the meeting, and ask that everyone present will approach the meeting in a spirit of cooperation.

Exercise caution in your business affairs, for the world is full of trickery. But let this not blind you to what virtue there is. Many people strive for high ideals, and everywhere life is full of heroism.

Desiderata

BUILDING UNITY & A TEAM THAT EXCELS

A Shopping List for Kosovo

The power of light has much to teach us about building a team that can accomplish great things.

Jane Clapham directs the Life Foundation's youth programmes. Dynamic, enthusiastic and always ready for a new discovery, she recounts the effect the World Peace Flame had on our first extended youth retreat. Consider the transformational power of taking a group of people through an authentic experience within the real world.

Half way through our first ever three-week Youth Event at our mountain centre in North Wales, I found myself sitting in a circle with eighteen youth leaders from all corners of the globe.

I had a challenge to offer them.

It was August 1999, immediately after the Peace Flames had come together. The experience had been so powerful for the young people that we had kept a light from the Peace Flame burning during all our sessions. It had become a constant reminder of our goals, a window out onto the world we all wanted to help transform. We all felt it had made a big difference to the group. But how real was this difference? Circumstances had given me the perfect way to find out.

The previous night I had received a call from my step-father, Frank. He was in trouble. He had volunteered to drive a lorry load of aid to the former war zone of Kosovo for a Welsh charity, and their normal supplier of tinned food and medical supplies had let them down at the last minute. Could we help?

Many of the young people present in the room knew suffering from first-hand experience. They were from the violent streets of Cape Town, the mountains of Ecuador, the war zones of the North Caucasus and from across Europe, the Pacific and the Americas. They were highly motivated young people who had come to us because they wanted to make a difference.

I put Frank's predicament to the group. Would they like to make an enduring contribution to peace, right here and now in North Wales?

It couldn't have come at a better time. With each day of the retreat we had all experienced a great power of confidence and strength building up, both as individuals and as a group.

Their response was immediate. They couldn't wait!

Within hours they had agreed on a plan and formed themselves into action teams. They spent the next three days in intense activity. They contacted local supermarkets, created leaflets and press releases, organised transport and arranged interviews with the local radio and newspapers. Fired with vision, they were not going to accept anything less than complete success. Arrangements were made to collect food at local supermarkets at the end of the week.

On the appointed day, we arrived at supermarkets in the nearby towns of Bangor and Caernarfon with mountains of leaflets and empty banana boxes. Standing by the entrance, the young people took turns to give out 'Shopping Lists for Kosovo', asking shoppers to buy just one extra item and deposit it for shipping off to Kosovo. Gradually, their pile of donated food began to grow.

The experience was both challenging and enlightening. Sometimes, seemingly affluent shoppers would brush them aside while poorly dressed families often brought large quantities of goods. Elderly Welsh grandmothers who obviously had hardly a penny to spare would come up to them with bags full of food and tears in their eyes. All day long we heard hundreds of variations on the remark, 'Thank you for giving us this chance to help those poor people in Kosovo.' People had wanted to give. We gave them the opportunity.

By the end of the day the pile of food had grown into a mountain weighing more than 7.5 tonnes. As the young people took turns to load Frank's truck, their eyes shone with pride in their accomplishment. They knew this food would soon be keeping hungry people alive in a war-torn land.

Perhaps most exultant of all was a youth leader named Mourad from the Russian North Caucasus. His homeland had itself been ravaged by war. 'Where I live I am usually at the other end of this food,' he said, almost beside himself with excitement. 'Aid trucks like this *come* to our village, and I know just how the people receiving this food will feel. It means someone far away thinks of you and cares for you. Just knowing this can give you the strength to keep going.

'Today,' he continued, 'I have been at the other end of the journey. It's shown me how kind people are and that when you are determined to make a difference, you really can. I am so amazed at how great it feels to be *giving* the food!'

The day was a turning point for Mourad. He had come to Wales quite unsure of his future, wondering whether to help with refugees in his homeland or just get on with his career. Now he was certain.

On his return, Mourad went straight to work. Two years later, he had become a key leader in local relief efforts, running food distribution programmes for several thousand displaced families, co-ordinating a number of schools and doing everything he could to ensure the safe passage of humanitarian supplies.

He was twenty-three. His life as a peacemaker had begun.

Jane Clapham, North Wales

*The example of a flame, which shines equally **on all** and **in all**, gives us the keys to turn a group of empowered individuals into a joyful, enthusiastic team capable of anything.*

❖ *Just as every flame removes darkness, so every individual has a valuable contribution to offer, no matter how large or small.*

❖ *Two flames brought together always add to each other's light. They never subtract from each other. In just the same way, a group will achieve phenomenal results when everyone within it takes care only to add to each other's efforts.*

❖ *We observe that light shines furthest when it is concentrated into a beam. Likewise, the outcome will be most far-reaching when everyone in the group pulls together to achieve a common goal.*

A Team Creates Its Leadership

Calm, respect and compassion are usually the least likely states you'd expect to encounter in a modern office that has become fractured by intense conflict.

Nevertheless, our very human ability for care and appreciation is never far below the surface. Often, all that is needed to restore harmony and enthusiasm in a team is the simple reminder of our respect for each other as human beings. Here is how one woman turned around a disastrous leadership problem in her office.

A few years ago I had begun a habit of lighting a World Peace Flame candle every day. It soon became an important feature of my life, and I particularly noticed how it introduced a very calming and stabilising presence during times of stress or conflict.

One of these occasions was when crisis enveloped the humanitarian aid organisation in which I work. There had been a change of leadership, several long-term members of staff had departed and important deadlines loomed that were critical for our organisation to continue receiving government funding.

For some reason, the new Director could not seem to understand the importance of these deadlines. Despite being repeatedly informed of the situation, he constantly diverted staff to work on other tasks. Our experts in overseas aid were accused of insubordination if they requested that staff be allowed to do the work for which their projects paid them. An air of panic and desperation enveloped the office as deadlines loomed nearer and we were unable to complete the required documentation. Within a few weeks the situation had become so dire that all the staff except one had resolved to leave and find other jobs.

One day, acting on a hunch, I decided to start bringing the World Peace Flame into work. I explained all about it to my colleagues and placed it in a central location within the office. Each day it would sit on the desk from morning to afternoon, a small flame quietly burning within a miniature miner's lamp.

I cannot explain why the effect of this simple action was so dramatic. Perhaps it is because millions of other people are lighting flames for peace from a candle just like this. Perhaps their positive influence made a difference in my office. Or perhaps it was because I wanted so much to bring back a sense of peace to my colleagues. Whatever the cause, as soon as I brought the Flame into the office, everyone was immediately aware of a tangible harmonising influence.

Over a period of weeks, the attitudes of the staff began to change. 'The Flame helped us to focus clearly and calmly. It gave us a better perspective and enabled us to find solutions to our difficulties,' said one. Others described how 'we were able to see the Director as another human being', while all agreed that 'the Flame definitely influenced us to opt for a non-confrontational approach.'

As the days went by, I watched with amazement and more than a little gratitude as a sense of fairness, calm resolve and compassion arose within the staff as a unified whole. This attitude had a great influence on the Board of Directors in their discussions with the Director. As a result of our constant show of respect and refusal to give in to the urge for recrimination, he agreed to a voluntary departure.

The World Peace Flame had become the catalyst for an amazing transformation in our office. Over a period of only five weeks, instead of a situation that everyone says would have become 'very nasty', all the key project managers agreed to stay. A new Director was recruited who has since turned the organisation around.

Needless to say, I continue bringing the World Peace Flame into our office.

T.N., Australia

Erasmus said, 'Give light, and the darkness will disappear of itself.'

This story discloses several principles for healing conflict within an organisation.

❖ *It only takes one person to bring in the light. How empowering to discover that our single, individual effort might just be the necessary catalyst to resolve the entire situation!*

❖ *Light reminds us to look for solutions and to see everyone involved as a human being.*

❖ *By removing all insecurity, fear and panic, light rekindles our inherent respect for all.*

The World Peace Flame exerts a powerful harmonising influence. Countless people using it around the world tell us how conversations become more harmonious and 'win—win' within its presence.

If you want your office to have an effective, creative team atmosphere, then consider taking a World Peace Flame into work.

The Fellowship of the Flame

In this lyrical description of the beauties of Snowdonia, North Wales—the area of Britain that is home to the World Peace Flame—you will discover how walking with a flame can bring unity to a whole region of diverse communities. Here, the warden of the area describes for us his impressions of a project he instigated recently.

E very New Year's Eve, the ancient stone walls and mossy roofs of the little village of Beddgelert are lit by the blazing light of its Millennium Beacon, a great bonfire first kindled as part of many beacons lit across the UK for the Millennium. Beddgelert lies in the very heart of Snowdonia, North Wales, a rugged land of lakes and mountains where tales of heroes, giants and dragons seem to fall upon you from every rocky precipice and every tree-clad shoulder.

When I heard about the plans for the Millennium Beacon, I immediately thought of lighting it from the World Peace Flame, which has its home in a similarly ancient valley on the other side of the region. The World Peace Flame was created here in Snowdonia when Flames were brought from the four corners of the world. I felt it would be so exciting if communities from the four corners of Snowdonia could carry World Peace Flames over the mountains to ignite the great beacon of light in Beddgelert.

In my work as warden of Snowdonia National Park I am intimately in touch with the varied communities that nestle within its ancient valleys. A few telephone calls and a day or two later, we had our plan. The Fellowship of the Flame was born. Four walks would carry four World Peace Flames to light the Beacon at Beddgelert. It would be a symbolic act of unity serving to bring a whole region of scattered communities together.

A few days before New Year's Eve, 2000, seventy people from all over the region gathered at the Life Foundation's Centre in the north of the Park for an evening dedication. As we watched the World Peace Flame ignite the four Welsh miners' lamps that would accompany the walks, a profound silence and joy settled upon us. A young girl from Caernarfon wrote later, 'Nobody in the world has ever given me a present as beautiful as that, not even Santa.'

We were ready to begin our journeys.

The first Flame was carried by a local mountaineering club, which includes some of the toughest guys in the region. They planned a non-stop, hard-man expedition direct from the village of Bethesda, up over the peaks of the mighty Glyderau, down into the next valley, over Mount Snowdon itself and finally down its south-western flank into Beddgelert.

Wild weather caught them as they passed through the Castell-y-Gwynt (Castles of the Wind) on the top of the Glyderau. Fields of upthrust crags sounded like organ pipes in the ferocious wind and snow, creating a wild melody of mountain and sky that played around their lamp. Finally, despite their best efforts, a particularly strong gust of wind blew out their Flame of Hope. 'What will the others say when they hear about this?' they asked, looking at it disconsolately, wondering if all hope for peace had also gone with the Flame's extinction. Eventually, they succeeded in re-igniting it by huddling together in the lee of a big snow-covered boulder, and so pressed on with their journey down to the saddle where I was to join them. They met me with much fumbling for words, eventually confessing the worst with shame in their eyes.

I laughed heartily and explained that the Flame of Peace is an essence that you carry, that its hope is stored in its wick, and that their concern would certainly have kept this alive during their walk.

As they continued, they found—as did all the walkers who carried the Flames—that the highlights of their journey were the conversations they had along the way. Can you imagine a group of tough mountain men walking the precipitous crags of the well-known PyG track up Snowdon, carrying a lit flame as carefully as if it were a baby? 'What on earth are you doing,' every passer-by would ask in amazement, 'carrying a miner's safety lamp which is meant to be underground, up here on top of a mountain, alight, in the middle of the afternoon…?' Most expressed grave doubts about the group's sanity!

However, each interaction gave the men a chance to talk about the Peace Flame, its extraordinary origin, and all that it represents. They watched every person they met become deeply moved and inspired by their purpose, and gradually began to realise the power of their walk. Everyone wants peace, they found. Furthermore, the men were beginning to appreciate how much they themselves could do. They began to realise that although they personally would only travel less than a score of miles, their many conversations along the way would eventually broadcast their peace message out for thousands of miles.

The team walking from Betws-y-Coed had similar experiences on the way up to the famous Pen-y-Gwryd hostelry where Sir Edmund Hilary stayed while training his 1953 Everest Expedition. From there the Flame was taken down the rugged head of the Nant Gwynant (Valley of the White Stream), past the rushing waterfalls where the River Glaslyn tumbles off the slopes of Snowdon. It stayed overnight in the little village by Llyn Gwynant (Lake Gwynant) and was then carried by canoe across the lake and downriver to Beddgelert.

It is a rare experience for the people in these tiny, ancient villages to feel they are taking part in something of global significance. Yet, when the opportunity came they participated with their whole hearts. As they paddled the Flame across the lake, the young daughter of one of the families cradled it in the front of her canoe with great love and affection. Declaring she would guard it at all costs from falling into the water, she remained undaunted even after one of the other canoes capsized in the freezing conditions!

A third Flame was carried in relays from the Life Foundation's Course Centre over the hills to the adjacent Llanberis Valley and then up over the northern ridges of Mount Snowdon. Each time you set off into the mountains from a valley floor in Snowdonia you wonder what dramas the region's fickle weather will provide. On this day the team set off in miserable sleet and rain, only to find the clouds dissolving to reveal a magnificent arch of deep blue sky. As they changed teams at the ridge top, surrounded by glorious sparkling, snow-covered mountains, one of them began the old Yiddish peace song 'Shalom Shaveram'. Soon, the whole group was singing in harmony, sky, song and the World Peace Flame combining to create an explosion of unity between them all and the wide world around. It was exhilarating!

Later, the Flame rested overnight in the little hamlet of Rhyd Ddu. 'The travelling Flame nestled within our circle of mountains,' wrote the guardian of the Flame that night. 'The ghosts of the old mill whispered their appreciation. The Flame, carefully placed in a window, cast its yellow glow into the moonlit mountain garden. Hopefully it travelled beyond, in the dead of night... Wishfully it did its rounds and its message was subconsciously received...' It arrived in Beddgelert the next morning accompanied by community members ranging in age from two to seventy-nine!

The final Flame departed from the Croesor Valley in the south of Snowdonia and made its way down through old-growth woodlands onto narrow tracks around the Matterhorn of Snowdonia, Mount Cnicht. This team travelled through a land steeped in history, along paths that have been used for millennia. What would the quarrymen of old have thought to see a group of people passing by with a lighted Flame for peace? Very likely, amidst the hardships of their tough and difficult lives, they would scarcely have conceived that people would one day walk for pleasure and friendship through their land. Yet now our group of thirty Croesorians walked with joy through the vast and empty landscape. Few actually witnessed the passing of the Flame, just as few of us appreciate the daily passage of the sun. Yet in the wake of the sun we find the essential energy of life, and in the wake of the Flame there was peace. As we walked, we had time to reflect on how precious peace is.

In fact, at the end of our walks we found that all of life is precious. On New Year's Eve, a brave young girl named Dilys was carefully escorted to the side of the Beacon. Diagnosed with a brain tumour that gave her only weeks to live, she took a torch lit from the four Flames and held it to the pyre. Soon, her face was etched in unforgettable joy by the light of the flames of this great beacon of peace. The firelight and the moon's rays seemed to combine and the shadows of people mingling around the village seemed to be dancing in unison. The light of peace had brought a whole region together in friendship.

Something happened that evening that healed us all. Dilys lived on for more than eighteen months, inspiring everyone with her courage and enthusiasm for life. The men from the mountaineering club still walk with the Flame of Peace every New Year and people across the whole region of Snowdonia have discovered how easily they can make a contribution for peace.

S.R., North Wales

Creating walks for peace with the World Peace Flame is one of the fastest ways to bring unity to your area. All you need is a lamp, some fuel, a good supply of home-baked cookies, and a plentiful quantity of smiles. Please tell us about your experiences!

> *Even as drops of water make the ocean, so we too, through friendship, can become an ocean of friendliness. The shape of the world would indeed be transformed if all of us lived in a spirit of love and amity with one another.*
>
> Mahatma Gandhi

How Do You Forgive a War?

What can you say to someone whose heart and family and liveli-hood have been torn asunder by tragedy? At these moments there are few words, few thoughts that can help. Yet actions can heal, when all the talking has ceased. In this story we see how one woman who caused great pain was able to go on and instigate even greater healing.

It was the end of an extraordinary retreat.

Andrew and I were sitting in a circle with a group of women aid workers in Bihac, Bosnia. With the World Peace Flame burning by our side, we had just been through a week of profound healing and transformation.

It was late 1999, only three years after the end of the war, and our retreat had been the first time that the UN had invited Serbs, Croatians and Bosnians to be together under one roof. Tensions, at times, had run understandably high.

Nevertheless, we had witnessed profound moments of healing during the week. Days of nurturing therapies and new insights had worked their magic and eventually the women had broken through years of pain into an experience of real respect for each other.

Now, as we sat together, I felt sure they were ready to take a new and greater step… into forgiveness.

We gave them each a candle lit from the World Peace Flame and I related how its inspiration had come in part from people just like them, mothers and daughters who had also lived through war. Gradually, I felt their hearts begin to reach out towards others who had suffered like themselves.

With this change, I began to sense a very deep stillness entering the room.

From that deep well a Bosnian doctor gently broke into the silence. She described how the week had brought her such great healing that she wanted to give something back to the group. Speaking softly, yet with passion, she began to share one of the most important turning points in her life.

After the war ended she and her husband had decided to go to the coast of Croatia for a time, hoping to recover from the immense trauma of losing their son in the fighting.

One day, she said, she was sitting on the sand gazing despondently out to sea, absently letting handfuls of sand slide through her fingers. At one point, something stuck in her hand. It was a small shell.

In that moment, she continued, she had a spiritual experience that changed her life.

She felt the sea softly lapping against her feet, and the shell within her hand. As she looked from one to the other she realised that the ocean had carried this shell to her. The very water that had carried this shell was also connecting her to other continents. The same ocean she sat by connected her with children suffering in Africa. The water touching her feet would also be touching theirs.

In that moment she knew that she was not meant to be sitting on a beach on holiday. Even though she had lost her own son, there were children back at home who needed her. Desperately. Her life could still have meaning.

'I got up from the beach,' she recalled, 'went back to the hotel and found my husband. 'Let's go home,' I said to him. The strange thing was that he was feeling exactly the same!

'Since that day,' she went on, 'I carry that shell with me everywhere, as a reminder of my purpose.' She looked around the room and her voice choked for an instant. 'It would make me very happy if I could pass it round this group so that you could all add your prayers to it. Maybe it will help you too.'

With tears rolling down her cheeks, she reached into her pocket and pulled out the shell. Holding it tightly for a few seconds she then passed it to the woman on her right.

As she did so, a large Serb woman got slowly and deliberately to her feet. She had been the focus of many painful moments of conflict and anger during the week, and we drew in our breath as she began to walk across the room. Was it possible she might kindle yet more pain?

Nevertheless, I felt a certainty within my heart. I felt sure that whatever she was about to do would be okay.

Slowly, oblivious to everyone else, she went over and knelt down behind the Bosnian woman.

She reached out and put her arms around her Bosnian colleague, hugging her closely. Huge tears began to fall from her eyes, saying more than words ever could.

A deep transformation was taking place within her. She raised her head and looked long and slowly round the whole group before closing her eyes and saying gently, over and over again, 'I'm sorry. I'm so sorry.'

Her words tore apart every boundary in the room.

Suddenly, Muslims were hugging Christians, Bosnians embracing Serbians—there were no barriers. In that moment there were no different religions, no different countries, no different sides. Instead of meeting at the level of differences, the women rose to another level where they met as mothers. As mothers they knew and understood the pain of losing a child. As mothers they knew in their hearts that to hate is not the way. As mothers they just wanted to love. Simply and humanly to love.

They had made the next step. They had discovered forgiveness, a forgiveness so complete it crossed every wall and healed every heart. They were no longer Bosnians, Serbians or Croatians. They were friends. And they were ready to begin the work of healing their country together.

In that moment I learned the power of forgiveness. I learned how the act of reaching out and taking the first step—no matter who is right or who is wrong—takes us into a realm where judgements are forgotten and healing is instant.

We looked around the room. There was no longer any real need for words. With the help of the Peace Flame we had all become one, and that was enough.

Savitri MacCuish

PART 3

PRACTICAL WAYS

To Use the World Peace Flame

" Many candles can be kindled from one candle without diminishing it. "

The Midrash

USING THE WORLD PEACE FLAME

Ⓦ One Small Act Per Day

ⓌLighting New Candles from the World Peace Flame

ⓌWorld Peace Flame Groups

ⓌA Talisman for Self Empowerment

MEDITATIONS WITH LIGHT - FOR HEALING CRISES
AND ACHIEVING DREAMS

ⓌThe World Peace Flame Meditation
to bring peace to yourself, your family,
your workplace and the world

ⓌWhat Should I Do Next?
a source of guidance for every moment

ⓌPlease Reveal Yourself to Me
to access your untapped strengths

ⓌIs There Anyone There Who Can Help Me?
gaining a friend who can guide you in times of need

USING THE
WORLD PEACE FLAME

" *What is true of the individual will be tomorrow*
true of the whole nation if individuals
will refuse to lose heart. "

Mohandas K. Gandhi

Using the World Peace Flame

A candle lit from the World Peace Flame is your simple, quick, go-anywhere method for letting go of all the complicated 'busy-ness' of life. It helps you regain peace of mind and that marvellous feeling of being equal to every situation you encounter.

Just lighting it makes a difference!

When you receive such a candle, we invite you to do two simple things:

1.   *Light it*—for your family, yourself or for the world.

2.   *Pass it on*—light other people's candles from yours.

(If you do not know someone who can give you a World Peace Flame, you can obtain one from the addresses at the end of the book.)

You might then like to pause for a few moments by its light. Let yourself relax into a welcome pool of calm.

We call these 'moments for inner potential'. This kind of breather is like making an appointment with yourself amidst a busy schedule. It will give you space to relax, recharge, and re-evaluate what is important to you at this moment—and what is not.

Many people who use the World Peace Flame stop and light their candle several times a day. No athlete would attempt to exercise all day long without any break. Why then, should we?

With regular practice, you will find your time with the World Peace Flame helping to bring out your greatest strengths and talents in every situation you encounter in life.

Light the World Peace Flame when you want to:

- ❖   Pause and let go of stress

- ❖   Relax and recharge your batteries

- ❖   Send healing thoughts to someone you care about

- ❖   Make an important meeting go smoothly

- ❖   Be more creative—or pass an exam

- ❖   Resolve a conflict with someone

- ❖   Send healing to where there is a natural disaster or a war

- ❖   Tell someone you love them

- ❖   Sing Happy Birthday

- ❖   Say 'I'm Sorry,' 'I'll do better next time' or perhaps 'I really care about you' or even, 'I do!'

- ❖   And don't forget to send out a prayer or affirmation for peace. The world needs your light!

When you light your World Peace Flame candle, you might like to remember that thousands of others will have been lighting a candle just like yours on this day. When you need some help, draw strength from this web of light. And when you have some light to spare, give some back.

One small act per day -
Lighting the World Peace Flame

If you think about the people whose stories are in this book, you'll realise that their lives changed because they *used* the World Peace Flame and/or the power of light. Don't let your candle gather dust on a shelf; rather, fill your house and your life with its light.

You will find that one small, positive act per day can be enough to affect your perception of life—and therefore your whole experience of relationships, your work and yourself.

As the stories in this book show, the simple act of lighting a Flame at the start of each day can be the first small step towards a great leap forward in your life.

In the next section, we've included some meditations which people have found effective when sitting in front of the World Peace Flame.

Lighting new candles
from the World Peace Flame

You can light someone else's candle from your own in an instant. Passing on the World Peace Flame is as easy as that.

We suggest that you let the new candle burn for two or three minutes next to the original candle before you put either of them out. During that time, think of how much you would like to see peace in the world and in your own life.

Remember to light a new candle for yourself before your initial one burns away!

World Peace Flame Groups

One of the greatest contributions we can all make to peace in the world is to gather people together to build circles of friendship, positivity and trust.

World Peace Flame Groups give you an easy format to do

this. Simply gather a small group of friends or colleagues together for an hour or so at somebody's house to give each other support and friendship and study new insights into living a more empowered life. Many groups discuss new ways to build a better ambience within their family life, workplace or community.

You might like to adopt the following format, which is being used by World Peace Flame Groups around the world.

- ❖ Start by focusing for a moment on peace—a more abundant, interesting, caring, expressive life for all—using a favourite poem, song, quote or prayer.

- ❖ Use the World Peace Flame meditation together for five minutes or so (see page 258).

- ❖ Read from an inspiring book or watch a segment of an inspiring video together for ten to fifteen minutes.

- ❖ Spend 20—30 minutes giving everyone the chance to share an insight or relevant experience.

- ❖ Finish with a song, prayer, inspiring reading—or just silence.

- ❖ Enjoy a few minutes catching up with each other over your favourite refreshments.

The World Peace Flame offices can give you many more ideas if you would like help with the activities or structure of your sessions. You can get help in finding contacts close to your area from the addresses at the back of this book or, alternatively, visit:

www.worldpeaceflame.com

A Talisman for Self Empowerment

Are you excited by the possibilities of how great life is when you are full of energy, self esteem and positive charisma? Here is a Talisman—a quick reminder—to help you stay that way.

❖ *Your waking moments define your day.* Try starting each day with a proactive, energising meditation—even while you are still sitting or lying in bed (see page 265).

❖ *Catch the morning tide.* From the moment you get up, engage with nature's morning current of dynamism and vitality. In every action be creative and stay happy, excited, joyous and centred. Aim to lift every person you meet—starting with yourself!

❖ *Practise highly positive self-talk.* Our minds are always full of chatter—and often the speakers are fear, anxiety, lack of self worth or frustration. So instead, call in the 'good guys'! Get into the habit of asking yourself positive questions. What are your strengths? What do you like about your life? What proactive step could you take towards your goal—at this moment?

❖ *Enthusiasm is contagious.* So are depression and negativity. What kind of people do you spend most of your time with?

❖ *Do you want to be right—or happy?* Did you know that judgement diminishes your power and creativity? Try looking at everything uncritically for an hour, and see how you begin to feel more positive about your life. In conversation, observe what's being said and aim to deflect the discussion away from condemnation and negativity and towards openness and creativity.

❖ *Listen to your inner mentor*, the quiet part that knows the right step to take next. Keep yourself free of greed, fear and despondency, which contaminate your ability to hear this amazing source of wisdom we all have within.

❖ *Call gratitude to the rescue.* When you're feeling down, one of the fastest ways back up is to write a 'grateful list'. Note your successes, no matter how small. 'I had a great warm shower this morning.' 'My dog was wagging her tail this morning, she was so pleased to see me.' When you start with the small or humorous, you'll soon find everything has its positive side!

❖ *What is your purpose?* The higher the purpose you serve, the greater the benefits life brings you. For example, adopt the attitude that your work/career is not just for yourself, but for your family. And not just for your family, but for your community, or… for the world.

❖ *Walk on a path you've never walked before.* Try at least one act of spontaneous creativity or dynamic risk-taking per day. It is one of the fastest ways to high self esteem.

❖ *Energising your body energises your mind and emotions.* Eat fresh, high vitality, cruelty free food. Try walking as often as possible—and not just all the way to the car! Have you ever slept under the stars in your garden?

❖ *Perform one small positive act per day.* Pause to light a World Peace Flame each day, preferably in the morning. Decide which of the points in this Talisman you are going to act on during the day. In the evening reflect, without condemnation, on what you have achieved. If you feel you would like to have done things differently, simply visualise yourself doing it a new way next time.

Few of the insights here are hard to implement, none of them take much time. Yet combined they could give you immense new reserves of energy, vigour, happiness and creativity.

Remember...
...it only takes one person to change your life—and that is *you!*

MEDITATIONS WITH LIGHT

FOR HEALING CRISES AND ACHIEVING YOUR DREAMS

" Learn to get in touch with the silence within yourself and know that everything in this life has a purpose. "

Elizabeth Kubler-Ross

Meditations with Light

L ight meditations are one of the easiest and fastest tools for quickly regaining your mental vitality, enthusiasm and focus. They are virtually free—you only need a candle—and can be done almost anywhere, at any time, without the need for any other props.

Have you noticed how much more effective you are when you are happy and in tune with yourself? We are at our best in life when we maintain our own natural balance between an inward focus and an outward expression, between building our inner resources and expending energy in our hectic lives.

The majority of us spend most of our days in out-going activity. Light meditations are an easy way of regaining our balance.

Here are some simple guidelines to help you make the most of your meditation.

❖ If you are tired or low in energy, have a quick shower or go for a short walk before you sit down.

❖ Above all, be comfortable. Often, people like to wear loose-fitting clothing made of natural fabrics. Most people prefer to sit in an uncluttered environment.

❖ Leave the rest of your life outside the door. Enjoy these moments that you have set aside for yourself.

❖ Sit on a chair with your back straight and your legs uncrossed or sit cross-legged on the floor. Place your candle in a position where you can look at its light without straining your eyes or neck.

❖ In the first few moments when you are sitting, just focus generally on your flame or your breath, without introducing the distraction of a specific goal.

❖ If you are using a candle, make sure you follow the general safety guidelines in the Appendix.

❖ Remember to smile! Light meditations are designed to help you see how beautiful life is. Be open to the deeper joyfulness that bubbles up from within.

If thoughts come…

…(as they will!) try to step back and let them pass. We all experience a constant stream of thoughts, and getting caught up in each one is a little like standing in a queue of people. While you are in the line, you can only see the people immediately in front or behind you. If you step to the side of the line, you can see where you have come from, and where you are going.

Thoughts are like this. They pass in an endless line, and when our attention is engaged with each thought it is very hard to be aware of any other perspectives. Yet there is more to ourselves than our thoughts. Einstein said we only use 10% of our minds. The other 90% is more purposeful, wise and free than the everyday 'chattering' mind we are so familiar with.

Stepping aside from the endless stream of thoughts enables you to get in touch with this part of you. You will find that it is untroubled by the ups and downs of thoughts and emotions. It is filled with unparalleled strengths.

Meditation and contemplation help you step out of the line of thoughts so you can get in touch with this greater part of yourself.

The World Peace Flame Meditation

This meditation helps you find peace, heal conflicts or send thoughts of healing to a person or situation needing it, including yourself. Peace starts with ourselves—if we are at peace with ourselves, we are more able to help others find peace. This meditation is being used by World Peace Flame Groups around the world as a way of bringing peace to every facet of life.

Level one - creating inner peace

1. *Dedicate:* this meditation to your own inner peace, or to any other person or situation that needs healing or peace.

2. *Relax:* sit comfortably for a few moments and gaze into the Flame. Focus on your breathing.

3. *Breathe:* take three deep breaths.

4. *Affirm: I Am Peace*
   on the next inhalation, quietly think 'I am peace.'

5. *Affirm: I Give Peace*
   as you exhale, quietly think 'I give peace.'

Repeat the affirmations as often as you like, and then relax into the vastness of peace that you have created with the World Peace Flame.

Level two - healing conflict

1. Relax for a few minutes and focus on your breathing, watching the natural rhythm of each inhalation and exhalation.

2. Imagine a situation in your life that needs healing— perhaps even yourself! Place an image of the situation in front of you at heart level, as if it were on a video screen.

3. As you breathe in, draw some of the stress or disharmony from the situation into your heart and immediately send it upwards and out of your crown as you breathe out.

4. Feel this stress or disharmony entering a beautiful golden cloud just above you. Visualise all of it turning into light within the cloud.

5. On an in-breath, draw this light down into your heart and breathe it out into the scene in front of you, bringing peace, ease and smiles to everyone there.

6. Repeat steps 2—5 until you feel *calm, free and re-energised with joy!*

There is a light that shines beyond all things on earth, beyond the highest, the very highest heavens. This is the light that shines in your heart.

Upanishads

What Should I Do Next?

This flame meditation helps you hear the moment-by-moment guidance your higher mind is constantly whispering inside you. You can add strength to the meditation by being in a slightly darker environment, with a flame burning in front of you as a single source of light.

1. Spend a few moments relaxing and focusing. You may want to systematically tense and relax parts of your body in time with your breathing—e.g. tense your legs as you breathe in, release the muscles as you breathe out, and so on throughout your body.

2. Feel that there is a beautiful, warming, glowing flame at the centre of your heart.

3. Imagine that your body has become the glow or aura around this flame. Let it become soft, golden and radiant. Try to feel, sense and visualise the reality of this experience.

4. Now take your awareness further outwards to the region around your body. Soften yourself and try to sense that you are surrounded by a very faint indigo light, just like the region which exists outside a candle flame.

5. In the silence and expansiveness of this awareness, let yourself become totally transparent, weightless and

warm. Become less bound by the world and its laws—on the earth, but not of it. Rest in the quiet stillness of this indigo light.

6.   Think of a situation for which you need guidance. Take a moment to make an inner request for help. Ask with passion and full purpose for answers that will enable you to take very positive steps towards achieving your goal.

7.   And then let yourself become silent. Let your awareness expand beyond the realm of the silent indigo light around you into a state of complete and utter stillness.

8.   Pause in this silence for a few minutes.

9.   Complete the meditation by bringing your awareness back to the presence of the flame within your heart. Then think about the presence of the flame in front of you and the room around you. Gently open your eyes.

Have a notebook and pen handy so that you can record any insights or ideas that have come for your next step.

Answers will come to you in this meditation, or during the day afterwards, if you give yourself permission to be open to your inner wisdom. If you stop a few times during the day for a moment or two, and remember your meditation and the request you made, it will help you to be open to these subtle promptings.

Please Reveal Yourself to Me

This interactive meditation helps make untapped strengths within the higher, greater part of your mind available to your normal, everyday mind. It also fills your body and mind with energy and enthusiasm.

1. Relax for a few moments, letting your breathing flow in an easy rhythm. Contemplate the light of the flame in front of you.

2. Introduce two stages into your in-breath, by pausing for an instant halfway before going on to complete the inhalation. Exhale in the normal way. Make sure you feel comfortable throughout, and that you don't breathe in more deeply than normal. Continue for three or four minutes.
    This stage helps energise your body and mind.

3. While you are doing this, focus on the flame in front of you. Feel as if its warm glow is like a friend or a special mirror that reflects a higher part within yourself.

4. Create a cycle of energy between you and the flame, taking your awareness towards the flame on your out-breath, and back from the flame on your in-breath.

5. Now, begin a phase of questioning. Breathe out through your mouth, saying out loud, 'Please reveal yourself to me.'

6. Repeat the phrase, out loud, on each out-breath. Don't worry if it feels a bit unusual or even silly at first! Speaking out loud anchors a strength and focus to your meditation that goes far beyond what we can normally achieve within our minds.

7. Observe the thoughts which come in response. You may find yourself emphasising different parts of your phrase, or other questions may arise, such as, 'Who am I?' 'Show me my purpose,' or 'How do I achieve my goal?' Say this instead on the out-breaths. You'll often find that a question leads to an answer such as, 'I am free,' 'I know who I am,' or 'I am a true friend to myself.' This may then lead you on to higher questions, and so on in an expanding cycle.

8. Continue for five minutes. If you find yourself losing concentration with these new phrases then go back to, 'Please reveal yourself to me,' as if it were an old friend.

9. Conclude your meditation by sitting quietly and relaxing for a minute or so. You may find it helpful to write down any insights that have come to you.

10. This meditation continues after you get up and carry on with your day! Its effects are often unbelievable. You may receive wonderful new insights, or cards or letters may come to you to confirm your experience, or you may open a book that gives you the answer to your question... Be ready for anything!

This meditation is designed to help you engage more deeply with life. Asking your question or repeating your phrase out loud is very important. Not only does it help you concentrate more fully on your question or answer, it also helps anchor the strengths that it brings from the higher mind.

The power of this meditation lies in helping to replace negative thoughts with spirals of ever greater and more exciting phrases, each one putting you more firmly in touch with the all-knowing, purposeful and joyful part of your mind.

> *All things embraced by His Light are freed...*
> *However far His Light illumines, Love penetrates, the Joy of Faith is attained.*
>
> Buddhist Chant

Is There Anyone There
Who Can Help Me?

This remarkable meditation is designed to bring you the experience of having a wise counsellor and mentor within, a source of wisdom to help you respond to the challenges of life. The meditation has three phases, one in the morning, one in the evening, and a third that will help you during every moment in between!

In the morning…

1. It is most effective to do this meditation as soon after your first waking moments as possible, either while still lying down, or sitting up in your bed. You may want to have a few good stretches before you begin.

2. As you breathe in, feel as if a stream of golden light is pouring into the crown of your head, down through the whole of your body and into your feet. Feel as if this golden light is flowing in from your highest self, God or a realm of infinite potential within you—use whatever language you relate to.

3. As you breathe out, feel as if a stream of dark blue indigo light is rising up from the earth, through your body and up to your crown. Allow your breath to be completely natural and free.

4. Continue this cycle of breathing for ten to fifteen minutes, making these two streams of light as real as you

can. Make their colours bright and rich, and feel that the light is so full and tangible that it seems like honey pouring through you. Aim to make the visualisation effortless, almost as if the two streams of light were breathing for you.

5. As you perform this meditation in the morning, the stream of golden light helps you gather the energy of dynamism that comes to us from the rising sun. The stream of deep blue helps you gather the qualities of patience, tolerance and unconditional nurture that come to us from the earth.

6. Affirm silently within yourself, 'May all my wisdom and intelligence now help me throughout this day.' Conclude your meditation by repeating this affirmation as powerfully as you can for three to four minutes.

During the day...

1. This meditation reaches its full potential when you help others during the day.

2. It seems a paradox to say that the times you most need help are the times to go furthest out of your way to help others. Nevertheless this is one of the greatest healing mechanisms known to humanity. Try to be available to help people a little more. Send letters to tell people how much you care, look for ways to make your relationships better, improve your workplace or do something for a friend.

3. As a result of your morning meditation, as you engage in the experiences of life, you will find that you have access to new and stronger sources of wisdom and creativity. You will find you communicate better, have better ideas and are more likely to say the right things at the right time.

In the evening...

1. Just before you go to sleep, spend five minutes repeating your meditation on the streams of light.

2. Then, make an affirmation that prepares you to go to sleep with *complete contentment:* 'I have done the best I can. May all the lessons I was supposed to learn today be completed in my sleep.'

3. Rest for a few moments with this feeling, knowing that within your unconscious mind you are generating a great strength that will help conclude any unfinished business during the healing hours of sleep.

4. Go to sleep with a deep feeling of contentment and calm.

Many people think we only receive deeply intuitive solutions to problems in times of great crisis but, in fact, the faculty to receive knowledge is available to us all the time. The three parts of this meditation cycle enable you to gain sensitivity and inner strength. Apply them during the day, and let them settle into completion during the night.

As a result, you create a day-by-day upward spiral that brings the quiet whispers of your inner wisdom closer and closer to the surface of your awareness.

> *The time has come to turn your heart into a temple of fire. Your essence is gold hidden in dust. To reveal its splendour you need to burn with the fire of love.*
>
> Rumi

THE ONGOING JOURNEY

THE WORLD PEACE FLAME AND YOU

> " *The future belongs to those who believe in the beauty of their dreams.* "
>
> *Eleanor Roosevelt*

The Ongoing Journey

As you can see from the quotes and stories in this book, the idea of passing on a flame of hope, though breathtakingly simple, has captured the imagination of people all over the world.

People everywhere are using the World Peace Flame to convey their friendship or love to family members, colleagues, friends and even strangers. We are hearing stories of the World Peace Flame being given to people in lands beyond where we have taken the Flame ourselves. And leaders of the world, including politicians in delicate peace negotiations, have drawn strength from its quiet calming presence. Business people bring it into their work places, inspiring executives to find solutions that will bring the greatest benefits to their staff and communities. It has become a symbol of hope and inspiration for quite literally millions of people.

Now, many of you who read this book will find it being installed in major cities and cultural centres in your countries.

The Hague, City of Peace

On 18th April, 2002, the World Peace Flame was installed as an eternally burning flame in front of the Peace Palace, home of the United Nation's International Court of Justice in The Netherlands. The inauguration ceremony brought together many diplomats from The Hague's international community, some from countries on opposing sides of current conflicts. Since then it has been providing a focus of peace for the hundreds of thousands of tourists who visit the Peace Palace each year. In fact, it is rarely seen without people sitting close by, drawing inspiration from the endless creativity of its flame.

The Legacy of Martin Luther King

On 27th September 2002, in Memphis, Tennessee, USA, the Flame was also installed in the National Civil Rights Museum, which commemorates the life of Martin Luther King and the Civil Rights Movement. Nearly one thousand people from all over the country welcomed the Flame, in a ceremony conducted in front of the very place where Dr King gave his life for his people's struggle for freedom. It now burns continuously in the Museum as a reminder of the progress humanity is making globally towards human rights. It helps us all remember that if we want a better world—it is up to us to create it.

Visit the home of the World Peace Flame, North Wales, UK

On 31st July, 2003, the original World Peace Flame was placed in a purpose-built monument at the Life Foundation's International Course Centre in North Wales. The spectacular four-metre high glass structure is set amidst the rugged mountains of Snowdonia National Park and celebrates the mother Flame from which all other World Peace Flames have been lit.

You are warmly invited to visit the World Peace Flame in its home, just as you are invited—wherever you may be—to light a World Peace Flame and pass it on to someone else.

As World Peace Flame monuments continue to be installed in the world's major cities, your activities with the Flame also make a big difference. Every time you pass on a Flame to another person, you create a momentary monument to a world at peace.

Mahatma Gandhi once said that he never expected the people of his non-violent movement to be saints. All he did was help them 'apply the law of love' a little more in their lives. The accumulated effect of millions of these individual efforts was enough to bring freedom to his country. In the same way, the positivity accumulated by passing on the World Peace Flame from one person to another adds up to an incalculable force for peace.

We look forward to meeting you somewhere along its journey.

At this moment in world history, what could possibly be more appropriately symbolic and inspiring than the placement of the first World Peace Flame Monument in front of the Peace Palace in The Hague? As dawn's light perpetually ushers in a new day for the Earth, with the fresh opportunities and hope that it brings, the ever burning World Peace Flame in The Hague reminds us that the nations and peoples of the earth have the power to choose and live Peace now!

S. G., Provost (Ret.)
National Cathedral, USA

Epilogue
The World Peace Flame and You

The World Peace Flame, above all, is a tool to inspire us all to think in new ways about how we can make our world a better place.

We are constantly receiving letters from people who have gained new insights from the World Peace Flame and as a conclusion to the amazing stories you have read in this book, we would like to leave you with some of their words.

May this treasury of inspiration help each one of us recall that there are no limits to the contribution we can make to the world our children will inherit.

****   ****   ****

The World Peace Flame is a beacon of hope that draws to it all those who hold the vision of a peaceful and loving world. The flame does not conquer the darkness, it simply shines its light and the shadows dissolve. And so, when we embrace the essence of the flame, the darkness in our lives is transformed, with the absence of force, into light.

K.S., Author, Canada

The best definition of peace I know is that peace is not the absence of war but the presence of humanity.

R. A., Author and Speaker, Canada

This is what Martin Luther King was all about. In a world torn apart in so many directions, let there be peace in all of us, let your Flame be eternal, let it reach us and may it forever shine.

M.S., Civil Rights Leader, USA

When I think of my experience with the World Peace Flame I am filled with the Light of Love and Peace. Now every flame I see is a reminder of the power of peace within each of us.

The World Peace Flame connects humanity by Light and offers a real sense of the possibility of Peace for all.

M.S., Minister, USA

The World Peace Flame allows me to take a troublesome look into the past and to see a bright light for the future.

A. M., Human Rights Commissioner, California

The World Peace Flame is both a noun and a verb; as a noun it symbolizes the human spirit's desire for global cooperation; as a verb it is part of the transformational process of consciousness that is making this desire a reality.

M.T., Attorney, Business Strategist, California

The World Peace Flame is a powerful symbol understood by people worldwide. The Flame has been cherished with care and will set countless hearts ablaze with the deepest love.

G.M., Abbot, The Netherlands

To me peace stands for the ability to come to terms with my own discontentment.

W.B., Conflict Resolution Co-ordinator,
The Netherlands

Never before in the known history of our human race have the flames of peace been brought together from the far corners of this world. The World Peace Flame, and the loving people who carry it forth in these dark times, remind us of our true home, the divine love inside of each of us. May the World Peace Flame shine brightly forever inviting peace back to our beautiful planet.

J.R., Publisher,
networking magazine, Canada

The World Peace Flame represents humanity's inevitable destiny of universal peace and keeps the light of this truth alive in our hearts as we advance.

S.P. & S.P., Founders, Healing Centre, USA

The power of the light that has been generated by the World Peace Flame has affected our hearts and thousands of others around the world beyond our imagination. May this light shine away any darkness in the world.

G.J. & D.C., Authors and Initiators
of International Attitudinal Healing Network

As I get farther down the road of peace I realize that God has provided me with a sense of humour. If a coincidence is God winking, and there is a constant flow of blessings from him, I just happen to have an umbrella up!
God is saying 'not so fast', do it 'half as fast'… And then I achieve my goals. Thank you for carrying this Light of Peace.

J.R., Radio Personality and TV Broadcaster, USA

The installation of a permanent Peace Flame at the International Court of Justice in The Hague is a major milestone in the history of a movement that is gaining considerable momentum throughout the world. At a time of significant global instability and when defence and security matters continue to dominate many countries' agendas to their detriment, we all need to re-focus on the critical importance of lasting peace both at the nation-state level and in the homes and lives of everyone throughout the world. I hope that all people who come in contact with the World Peace Flame... will be touched to reflect upon its significance for peace and healing so that their lives can be energised for the betterment of mankind.

P.A., Colonel, (Ret.), Australia

A single candle has expanded from a flicker of luminous light into a torch of hope. The glow from the World Peace Flame has entered into warring, distressed nations and healed troubled hearts... including mine. The World Peace Flame ignited my thinking that peace is possible.

P.B., General Manager
millionaire training programme, USA

The World Peace Flame is a beautiful symbol of the demonstration of the power of one tiny flame. That tiny light can allow a lost soul to find his way out of the darkest of places. The power of the Peace Flame comes from the love of those who carry it. You are that power... You are that light.

J.W. & K.B., Realtors, California

The World Peace Flame is symbolic of the dream of our universal social selves. Governments cannot give us peace. We earn peace when we allow it to manifest itself as a radiant glow in our hearts and evolve itself into the beloved global community. The World Peace Flame is a sacred reminder that only non-violence has the power to affirm, ennoble, heal and unite.

L.C., Faculty Dean and Minister, USA

We know that, even in these troubled times, the peace we are all seeking already exists within each of us. The light of the World Peace Flame serves as a constant reminder of that fact and can do the same for all people everywhere.

B.W., CEO, publishing house, USA

My family has personally experienced the gift of the World Peace Flame in our home.

From the first moment it graced us with its presence, I instinctively knew it wasn't 'just' a flame. I could *feel* its desire to connect with us. I could feel it had a consciousness. It was personal, tangible, unconditionally loving. It felt like a long-lost relative checking in on us, making sure that everything was okay.

Actually, everything wasn't okay. At the time, my husband and I were dealing with a severe situation that had trauma-tised the entire family. The repercussions could have been dev-astating. The Flame 'knew' we were in trouble and found us in our hour of need.

The appropriate remedy for the friction we had created was the restoration of peace, harmony and balance, all of which I am convinced the Flame carried into our home. We all felt the power of its presence as it sat serenely in our living room. I felt its strength of purpose, its caring, its determination to get through to us, its love and its desire to unify its children. In simplicity and silence, we were all touched and transformed by the Flame. The Flame needn't boast dogma or fanfare; it is the essence of grace.

The court case that loomed over us 'went away'. The legal system suddenly became infused with compassion and under-standing and the case was dismissed. The whole situation sim-ply disappeared—as simply as the Flame itself had appeared in our lives.

Instead of living in darkness and chaos, we have been blessed with the opportunity to reconnect with that river of love and intelligence that weaves its way through life. We recognise this blessing from the Flame and are eternally grate-ful to it and its keepers.

C.O., Actress, California

The innocence and dignity of one small flame gently reminds me how fragile and delicate is this peace inside each one of our hearts! The World Peace Flame represents that eternal silent voice within that whispers lovingly like a mother to her child, 'I am here, I am here.'

J.A., Director,
national network of mastery courses, USA

My husband, who suffers from depression, has found he gains solace from being in the presence of the World Peace Flame. He finds that when you're by yourself and have the World Peace Flame burning, it feels like it's a friend who watches over you and keeps you company.

T. N., Secretary, Australia

I make sure the Flame is alight every evening before I go to bed and it spreads such peace, love and harmony—a tangible feeling, as I turn the other lights off in the house knowing that it is spreading light up to and around, not just our own family but out to all the world. The warm glow it generates in me *has* to be real!!

W.S., Homoeopath, UK

My own personal experience is that the World Peace Flame has helped us as a family to ensure that meal times are relaxed and pleasant as we do not argue 'in front of the World Peace Flame'. It has pride of place on the kitchen table where we eat.

M.F., Community Leader, UK

Being together with the torchbearers of the Life Foundation is encouraging. I have never seen any difference between the way they carry out their work and the way they talk about it. They really implement what they say. For them world peace is a matter of heart.

P.E., Film Director, The Netherlands

The World Peace Flame mirrors the Light that is in each of our hearts where the truth of peace resides. It reminds us of who we are.

M.F,.CEO, art for peace company

Peace is a harmonious condition whereby purposeful, dynamic systems interact such that in the pursuit of each system's own development and process of self realization, none interferes with the ability of another system to pursue its own individual path, while, at the same time, optimizing, through their interactions, the underlying evolutionary conditions of the community of systems as a whole.

The inspiring work of the World Peace Flame epitomizes this condition.

M.B.E., President,
international environmental consultancy, New York

If only we could experience other people's lives and cultures first hand, we would understand how futile war is. For me, the beauty of the World Peace Flame is that it seeks to unite the diverse people of the world. Its light represents what could be possible if we open our hearts and perspective to be aware of the value of every human life and to see that love comes first.

L.R., Singer/Songwriter,
TV host and actress, USA

From the earliest times, humankind has gathered around a flame—for light, for warmth, for food, for community. We have shared our stories, our lives and our challenges around the circle of a fire. To me, the World Peace Flame symbolizes the best of humankind. It signifies the possibility and the potential for sitting together in a circle of peace, telling our stories, sharing our hearts and bringing light to the differences between us. Because, at the heart of it all, we are one family, one community, one people, and peace is the answer to every human challenge facing us today. May we all see the light of peace in our lifetime!

P.P., Senior Minister,
Church of Religious Science, California

Peace is a spiritual principle. You must apply the principle in every circumstance, relationship, task and transaction in order to achieve the result.

J.T., Author and Minister, USA

I was and continue to be deeply moved by the World Peace Flame and what it represents. I am so happy that this pro-peace emblem is burning around the planet.

H.D., Author, Director,
international training network

Through the light of the World Peace Flame I have seen the universal impact of vision and profound change. This light brings blessings and beauty to the core of each being where it has made a connection. Allow the Flame to touch your highest self and you allow your life to be forever transformed.

S.M., CEO, Therapist, USA

Face to face with the World Peace Flame, humanity will naturally reach out to serve the whole of creation. The Flame will naturally draw out of us the strength of love and compassion, and its nurturing force will heal the earth. The Flame is like an inner smile, a healing force for every human being. Offer your pain or suffering to the World Peace Flame and her love will pour out to you.

T.d.R, Media Liaison,
Psychotherapist, The Netherlands

The World Peace Flame is a powerful manifestation of humanity's inner urge to share the Divine Light and Divine Peace within them. May it burn brightly and spread rapidly to every person on Earth!

S.C., Director,
national healing association, USA

When I see the World Peace Flame I cannot discern the race, colour or culture that contributed to its beautiful, brilliant illumination. It is a simple, humbling reminder of life itself, of all things being contained in the light. We are the sparks that became the flame; we already are the peace we seek.

E.T., Co-director, Peace Ministry, USA

If only the world leaders would recognise the World Peace Flame and what it stands for. Human beings make the world what it is... let the Peace Flame burn brightly so all will come together to change the world for the better.

E.A., TV Broadcaster, California

We see the Flame as a tangible expression of an Intangible Manifestation.

P.&J.L., Former BBC producer &
Special Education Teacher, UK

May the power that is liberated by singing from our soul, contribute towards true world peace.

P.v.S, Conductor, The Netherlands

The World Peace Flame is the light which lights the light within.

L.M., Company Executive, Scotland

Lighting the World Peace Flame is a miracle. It makes us close to each other.

M.v.A,.Court Clerk, The Netherlands

May this monument reflect the flame that is burning inside each one of us. When you enter that inner space you will find peace and the feeling that every being in the universe is inter-connected. Knowing inner peace, you can co-create peace in the world outside.

H.v.d.S, Designer,
World Peace Flame Monument, The Hague

It's so exciting to be around the World Peace Flame. It guides me to live the life of my dreams. It reminds me of the beauty of the moment.

I.V., Founder,
network for financial professionals, The Netherlands

The World Peace Flame brings us to a point of inner peace, and connection with other peacemakers throughout the world.

T.L., Accountant, Glasgow

Live your Light; Shine your Light; be the Light and know it inspires and ignites the same in others.
What we believe we can achieve. Celebrate the path of this very special flame.

V.S., Founder,
partners of parliamentarians network, Australia

We all know that the sight of a campfire has the power to warm and cheer us, even before we enter its radiance. In the same way, the World Peace Flame not only warms and cheers, but gently enters our hearts, enabling us to carry its love and peace to share with others.

Australian Life Team

Light changes your life for ever. The challenges in life will still be there but you can change and act upon them with strength, courage, love and creativity. People will feel that in your presence they will want what you have; they will long for your peace and happiness.

H.d.W., *Dru Yoga Teacher, The Netherlands*

The most precious legacy we can leave for our children and their children is the pursuit of peace. It begins with an acknowledgement of the intrinsic worth of every human being and our increasing interdependence on one another.

R.S., *Director,*
citizenship education network, USA

Never choose to walk from light into the darkness. Always go from darkness to light until, standing in the light, you discover that there is really no difference between the two.

Q.W., *Social Worker and*
Life Foundation Volunteer Co-ordinator, The Netherlands

Having lived in Northern Ireland and Africa for several years, in places where it's easy to think you are surrounded by struggle and chaos, the World Peace Flame is an invaluable reminder that we have the choice of focussing on the light rather than the darkness.

Paulette Agnew
Director, Head and Heart Solutions; & Life Foundation Ireland

Light, like a small flame, exists within each of us. It is that which ennobles us and can be passed from person to person, filling the whole world.

Chris Barrington
Co-founder, Life Foundation

The World Peace Flame is a personal reminder to each one of us that 'you *do* make a difference.'

Kate Couldwell
Director, Life Foundation Midlands, UK

May all people of the world continue to strive for the highest good and realise the true purpose of their lives.

Rita Goswami
CEO, Life Foundation Australia

May the power of this light touch all those hearts in the world needing shelter, love, and friendship. May it awaken people to the presence of God in every being.

Anita Goswami
International Dru Yoga Co-ordinator, Life Foundation

The World Peace Flame acts as a reminder to each one of us to keep the inner flame of peace alight in each moment. The more we give to others and serve humanity, the brighter our light becomes.

Julie Hotchkiss
International Outreach Co-ordinator, Life Foundation

This Flame is a living witness to and a catalyst for the prayers of people all over the world. In its presence morality, conscience and liberty are awakened.

John Jones
Co-founder, Life Foundation

The World Peace Flame marks a point in history where science meets spirituality. Modern technology has advanced almost to the point where we are unable to use it wisely. Now, if there should be any further advancement, perhaps we should first develop our understanding of the power of the heart. Just as a flame does not judge who it shines on but rather casts its light equally in all directions, may this World Peace Flame act as a silent witness to compassion and kindness.

Savitri MacCuish
Executive Director, World Peace Flame Foundation

Light gives life to everything. In the darkness of the night, the world is lifeless. When the first rays of daylight appear, though, the whole world comes back to life. In just the same way it is how we look into the world that gives life and meaning to everything. We can look with light in our eyes and set free the inherent harmony, beauty, and purpose in all our gaze touches.

Mira Muller Grosse
Co-ordinator, Life Foundation Germany

May this Flame symbolising the unity of all beings bring hope and great strength to the people of this world, now and always.

Krishna Patel, (age 14)

When the World was created there were no natural boundary lines drawn across the land. It was all one land, one people, each born with the same right to live, work and prosper both materially and spiritually. There is no greater vision than unity, for we are all connected by the spirit of light. This is the first

World Peace Flame Monument to be established, and I believe that in our lifetime we will witness the establishment of such symbols in every major city in the world.

Mansukh Patel
Co-founder, Life Foundation

Peace is personal. It is about you and me, and how we embrace the qualities that make each of us unique, while also a part of the whole. May the World Peace Flame awaken each one of us to the potential of who we are and how we can create real peace in our world.

Chandra Rahman
Executive Officer, Life Foundation Australia

I believe that within each human being there burns a flame that shines as brightly as the World Peace Flame, and that flame has the potential in every moment to guide our thoughts, our words and our actions to bring peace to our world.

Louise Rowan
Executive Director, Life Foundation Canada

It takes one tree to make a million matches. It takes one match to set aflame a million trees. It takes one flame to set a million hearts ablaze with the light of peace: the World Peace Flame.

Shona Sutherland
Course Director, Life Foundation UK

We are entering an unparalleled era in history. Never before has there been a global dialogue about the legitimacy or illegitimacy of war, and whether or not we have searched for all possible peaceful solutions. The World Peace Flame helps us recall that peace is always possible when we make the effort to stand firmly, creatively and with respect for all.

Andrew Wells
Director, International Projects, Life Foundation

My Personal Reflections

Please use this page to write down your own inspirations
about how you can create a better world.

The World Peace Flame
has been presented to...

• His Holiness Pope John Paul II
• The Rt Hon. Tony Blair, Prime Minister of England
• Ujjal Dosanjh, Premier of B.C., Canada
• Kim Beazley, former Leader of the Australian Labour Party
• Sir William Deane, former Governor General of Australia
• Katrina Hodgkinson, State Member for Burrinjuck, NSW, Australia
• Herbert Fischer, former ambassador of East Germany to India
• Lord Mayors: Newcastle, Liverpool, Leeds, Birmingham;
  Wolverhampton; Lord Provosts of Aberdeen, Edinburgh (deputy),
  Inverness, Glasgow,
• Luciano Meira, Legion of Good Will, New York
• Emmy Lou Harris, singer, USA
• David Hayman, actor, UK
• Chaplain of The US Pentagon, Washington D.C.
• City Mosque, London, UK
• Coventry Cathedral, UK
• Father Maximillian Mizzi, Assisi, Italy
• Gedächtniskirche, Berlin, Germany
• Lichfield Cathedral, UK
• Arun Gandhi, MK Gandhi Institute for Non-violence, Memphis, USA
• Hon. Tony Benn, former MP, UK
• Pam Barratt, former MP for Edmonton, Alberta, Canada
• Dr Roman Herzog, former President of Germany
• Herb Gray, Deputy PM of Canada
• Westminster Abbey, London, UK
• World Parliament of Religions, Cape Town, South Africa
• Ralf Moeller, actor, Germany

- Jain Conference on Ahimsa, Delhi, India
- Rt Hon. Paul Murphy, Secretary of State for Wales
- The Rt Hon. Martin Bell, OBE, Member of Parliament, UK
- UNHCR, Bihac, Bosnia-Hercegovina
- Christopher Lee, actor, UK
- Daniel Arap Moy, President of Kenya
- Nana Mouskouri, singer
- Sir Bobby Charlton, Manchester United Football Club, UK
- Sir Bobby Robson, Newcastle United Football Club, UK
- Don Alejandro, Mayan Elder, Guatemala
- Gregory Smith, International Youth Advocate, Washington D.C.
- Jack Healey, former Director, Amnesty International, Washington D.C.
- James Gordon, Director of Presidential Commission for Complementary and Alternative Medicine, USA
- Metropolitan Police, London, UK
- St Laurenskerk, Rotterdam, NL
- St Mary's Chapel, Westminster Palace, London, UK
- St Francis Basilica, Assisi, Italy
- Kunzang Palyul Choling Tibetan Buddhist Monastery, Maryland, USA
- Swami Narayana Temple, London, UK
- His Holiness Saint Baba Bahar Singh Ji, Warwickshire, England
- Dr. Walther H. Lechler, Fellowship for Medicine of the Whole Person, Germany
- Dr Bertrand Piccard, Global Balloonist, Switzerland
- Wilda Spalding, World Wins Cooperation, Geneva, Switzerland
- Marshall Rosenberg, International Conflict Resolution Leader

... and many, many more

What Are Your Experiences with Light?

Many of the incidents you have read in this book have been contributed by people just like yourself. Their lives have been uplifted and transformed by their experiences with light, and they have shared their stories so others could benefit as well.

Perhaps you, too, have an experience you would like to share. It might be something that has happened to you personally, or an event relating to someone you know. Or you might know of poems, fables, legends or moments in history in which the power of light helped people transform their lives.

We are planning to print further volumes of empowering stories from the World Peace Flame, as well as publishing them on www.worldpeaceflame.com. So, if you have a story, please send it to us at:

World Peace Flame Stories
6670 AB Zetten
The Netherlands
worldpeaceflame@lifefoundation.nl
www.worldpeaceflame.com

Would you like the World Peace Flame presented in your Conference, Organisation or Centre? Presentations, lectures or retreats on the World Peace Flame and its ongoing work are available in many countries around the world. You can contact us at the addresses opposite for more information, as well as for details on our inspirational books, videos and audio products.

Contact Us

What are your ideas? What are your projects? In these times people all over the world are making the exhilarating discovery that creating positive contributions for the future depends on us all working together. You may be working on an amazing project that others could learn from. Or, you may have great ideas, resources or information that you aren't able to mobilise by yourself.

Either way, drop us an email or a letter and let's talk about it. You never know when sharing some thoughts together could catalyse another great project into being.

Continental Europe, Africa & Asia
World Peace Flame Foundation
Post Box 88, 6670AB Zetten, The Netherlands
Tel: +31 488 491 387, Fax: +31 488 491 930
Email: contact@lifefoundation.nl
www.worldpeaceflame.com

UK and Eire
Life Foundation International Course Centre
Nant Ffrancon, Bethesda, Gwynedd, LL57 3LX,
North Wales, UK
Tel: +44 1248 602900, Fax: +44 1248 602004
Email: worldpeaceflame@lifefoundation.org.uk
www.lifefoundationinternational.com

Australasia
Tel: +61 2 6161 1462
Email: info@lifefoundation.com.au
www.lifefoundation.com.au

The Americas
Tel: +1 604 263 4432
lifecanada@aol.com
usa@lifeworldwide.org

Savitri MacCuish

Global Ambassador of Peace, international speaker, retreat leader and author, Savitri draws from a rich and varied career spanning coaching, investment banking and instigating humanitarian projects. As one of the pioneers of the Life Foundation's war-zone detraumatisation work, Savitri has seen much suffering in the world. Her search for an authentic symbol of hope and peace has led her to become the prime instigator of the World Peace Flame and she is now Executive Director of the World Peace Flame Foundation and Life Foundation International (LFI). She has authored four books, produced numerous video tapes and CDs and features regularly in magazine and newspaper articles and on TV.

Savitri is International Director of Life Foundation Professional, training people in business and government in enhanced relationship and emotional management skills.

Dr Mansukh Patel

Scientist, philosopher, author and visionary, Mansukh is one of Europe's leaders in personal development and peacemaking. Famous for his unique blend of ancient and modern approaches to awakening the full potential of mind, body, emotions and heart, he has also become known as the 'Young Gandhi' by media in Europe.

Mansukh is a co-founder of the Life Foundation and of the World Peace Flame Monuments worldwide. He has instigated teaching Dru Yoga in the West and established Dru Yoga teacher training courses in seven countries. Subject of over 25 TV productions, he has produced more than 30 videos and numerous CD programmes, and is the author of 14 books, many of which have been translated into several languages. He leads over 130 workshops and 50 international lectures each year. Mansukh lives with his wife and three children in North Wales, UK.

Andrew Wells

International speaker, author, lifestyle trainer and detraumatisation expert, Andrew has trained people in thirty countries in whole-person approaches to health, self-empowerment and the healing of emotional trauma. He has 'walked his talk' in seminars and walking tours across thousands of miles of Continental Europe.

Andrew's professional background includes consulting engineering in Australia and working with the Quakers at their UN headquarters in New York. He now specialises in what he calls 'diplomacy of the heart', which has taken him into war-torn regions in the North Caucasus, Bosnia and East Africa. He has also been responsible for instigating a wide variety of humanitarian aid projects.

Andrew is the author of a wide range of videos, books and audio products on self-help and developing human potential.

The Life Foundation

The Life Foundation is made up of more than eighty therapists, health professionals, personal development trainers and others, who work worldwide to promote self-help approaches to health and well-being at every level of life.

The Life Foundation originated from a group of university students from diverse academic disciplines who, in the late 1970s, gained inspiration and practical wisdom from Chhaganbhai and Ecchaben Patel, Mansukh's parents, who had been part of Mahatma Gandhi's reform movement in India.

Today, the Life Foundation runs regular programmes of courses, seminars, retreats, conferences and humanitarian projects in ten countries on four continents, all aimed at helping people attain their highest potential. Life Foundation teams have trained people from the UN, leading businesses and health, educational and community groups worldwide.

Appendix - Using a Candle Safely

The use of light as a marvellous tool for accessing your inner strengths often invites you to light a candle flame or a lamp.

Please exercise your common sense at all times. Although it might seem that we are stating the obvious, please apply this list of safety considerations whenever you light a flame.

- ❖ Keep flames well out of the reach of all children and pets.

- ❖ Keep them on a heat-resistant tray and ensure that there is nothing around that could fall onto them.

- ❖ Keep all papers, curtains, clothing and any other flammable items well away from naked flames.

- ❖ Never leave a burning candle unattended.

- ❖ Do not place on electrical equipment such as televisions, or on fragile surfaces such as glass.

- ❖ Please do not light a candle for meditation or in any other situation if you are likely to fall asleep.

- ❖ Please obey all fire codes and restrictions that apply in your location.

The authors, the World Peace Flame Foundation and Life Foundation Publications cannot be held responsible or liable for any accidents caused by lighting candles or any other kind of flames.

THE SECRET POWER OF LIGHT

Dr Mansukh Patel

The moving account of one man's vision for peace. The story of the World Peace Flame unfolds and the transforming power of light is revealed. *The Secret Power of Light* is a marvellous blend of practical spirituality, scientific fact and profound understanding of the principles of light that govern our universe. In the same way as Einstein's Theory of Relativity revolutionised scientific thought, the Secret Power of Light as elucidated in this book promises to redefine your whole way of thinking.

£14.95   Hardback

GUIDE TO PERSONAL FREEDOM

Savitri MacCuish and Anita Goswami

Peace is a moment to moment process. As C. S. Lewis once said, "You cannot talk about peace with war in your heart." This book is a treasure-house of wisdom, a guide to your personal freedom. It shares important principles and techniques to re-create and nurture you, to redirect your life, to make it an expression of an inner revolution that is necessary to meet new challenges.

£7.50   Paperback

YOUR PERSONAL PEACE FORMULA

Dr Mansukh Patel

The Peace Formula offers fascinating new perspectives to enable us to achieve our highest dreams and ideals. This simple seven-point plan has been tried and tested in many different ways by some of the greatest people of our time. This Formula has the power to create lasting change that will ripple out into every aspect of your life, and beyond!

£8.95   Paperback

BELIEVE IN YOURSELF

Dr Mansukh Patel

An illuminating pocket-sized book in which Dr Patel explains how high self esteem and self confidence are inherent in us all. Practical ways to establish a powerful self-belief.

£3.75   Hardback

A CALL TO ACTION

Dr Mansukh Patel, Savitri MacCuish and Andrew Wells

Can we personally influence global terrorism, conflict in the Middle East and many of the other social, environmental and political crises of our time?

A Call to Action is a dynamic analysis of Gandhi's Seven Laws of Society, a model he created to address a society gripped by the same level of crisis we are facing today. Challenging, confronting, yet profoundly inspiring, this book shows us that we already have the strength and ability to help resolve the most challenging issues of our time.

The place to act is here.

The people that matter are the ones in front of us.

The time to act is now.

£9.99 Paperback

IMAGINE WORLD PEACE

Dr Mansukh Patel

Can you imagine World Peace? The tragic events of September 11th, 2001, have completely redefined our values and ideals. In this book Mansukh Patel invites us to expand our horizons to encompass a much greater celebration of life's diversity, respect for humanity, gratitude and compassion. Every aspect of our daily living affects everything else. This eight-week programme of daily exercises is based on the highly acclaimed *Your Personal Peace Formula*.

£2.50 Paperback

THE DANCE BETWEEN JOY AND PAIN

Dr Mansukh Patel and Rita Goswami

Your emotions contain a phenomenal power that can work either for or against you. This book is an essential manual for becoming the master of your emotions. It gives practical movements, breathing exercises and hand gestures (mudras) to effectively transform negative emotions into their positive counterparts.

£8.75 Paperback

All titles are available from your nearest Life Foundation address.

Prices are subject to change

YOUR PERSONAL NOTES